THE SOUND OF MUSIC

MUSIC BY *Richard Rodgers*

LYRICS BY *Oscar Hammerstein II*

BOOK BY *Howard Lindsay* AND *Russel Crouse*

The Sound of Music

A NEW MUSICAL PLAY

(Suggested by THE TRAPP FAMILY SINGERS *by Maria Augusta Trapp)*

Random House
New York

To
Maria and Mary

Photographs by courtesy of Friedman-Abeles and Toni Frissel

THE SOUND OF MUSIC *was first presented by Leland Hayward, Richard Halliday, Richard Rodgers and Oscar Hammerstein II at the Lunt-Fontanne Theatre, New York City, on November 16, 1959, with the following cast:*

(In order of appearance)

Sister Berthe, Mistress of Novices	Elizabeth Howell
Maria Rainer, a postulant at Nonnberg Abbey	Mary Martin
Sister Sophia	Karen Shepard
Sister Margaretta, Mistress of Postulants	Muriel O'Malley
The Mother Abbess	Patricia Neway
Captain Georg von Trapp	Theodore Bikel
Franz, the butler	John Randolph
Frau Schmidt, the housekeeper	Nan McFarland

Liesl		Lauri Peters
Friedrich		William Snowden
Louisa		Kathy Dunn
Kurt	Children of Captain von Trapp	Joseph Stewart
Marta		Mary Susan Locke
Gretl		Evanna Lien
Brigitta		Marilyn Rogers

Rolf Gruber	Brian Davies
Elsa Schraeder	Marion Marlowe
Ursula	Luce Ennis
Max Detweiler	Kurt Kasznar
Baron Elberfeld	Kirby Smith
Herr Zeller	Stefan Gierasch
Baroness Elberfeld	Maria Kova
A Postulant	Sue Yaeger
Admiral von Schreiber	Michael Gorrin

Neighbors of Captain von Trapp, nuns, novices, postulants, contestants in the Festival Concert: Joanne Birks, Patricia Brooks, June Card, Dorothy Dallas, Ceil Delly, Luce Ennis, Cleo Fry, Barbara George, Joey Heatherton, Lucas Hoving, Patricia Kelly, Maria Kova, Shirley Mendonca, Kathy Miller, Lorna Nash, Keith Prentice, Nancy Reeves, Bernice Saunders, Connie Sharman, Gloria Stevens, Tatiana Troyanos, Mimi Vondra.

Entire production directed by Vincent J. Donehue
Musical numbers staged by Joe Layton
Scenic production by Oliver Smith
Costumes by Lucinda Ballard
Mary Martin's clothes by Mainbocher
Lighting by Jean Rosenthal
Musical director: Frederick Dvonch
Orchestrations by Robert Russell Bennett
Choral arrangements by Trude Rittman

SCENES

(The story is laid in Austria early in 1938)

Act One

Act Two

MUSICAL NUMBERS

ACT ONE

Preludium

"The Sound of Music"   MARIA

"Maria"

      MOTHER ABBESS, SISTERS MARGARETTA, BERTHE, SOPHIA

"My Favorite Things"   MARIA, MOTHER ABBESS

"Do Re Mi"   MARIA, CHILDREN

"You Are Sixteen"   LIESL, ROLF

"The Lonely Goatherd"   MARIA, CHILDREN

"How Can Love Survive?"   ELSA, MAX, CAPTAIN

"The Sound of Music"   MARIA, CAPTAIN, CHILDREN

"So Long, Farewell"   CHILDREN

"Climb Every Mountain"   MOTHER ABBESS

ACT TWO

"No Way to Stop It"   CAPTAIN, MAX, ELSA

"An Ordinary Couple"   MARIA, CAPTAIN

Processional   ENSEMBLE

"You Are Sixteen"   MARIA, LIESL

"Do Re Mi"   MARIA, CAPTAIN, CHILDREN

"Edelweiss"   CAPTAIN, MARIA, CHILDREN

"So Long, Farewell"   MARIA, CAPTAIN, CHILDREN

"Climb Every Mountain"   COMPANY

ACT ONE

Scene One

Prelude.
Nonnberg Abbey. As the theatre darkens we hear the bells
of Nonnberg Abbey. When the theatre is completely dark the
sound of the bells fades and we hear feminine voices chanting
"Dixit Dominus."

SOLO

> Dixit Dominus Domino meo:
> Sede a dextris meis.

RESPONSE

> Donec ponam inimicos tuos,
> scabellum pedum tuorum.
>> *(In the darkness the curtain has risen and slowly the*
>> *lights come up on the interior of Nonnberg Abbey.*
>> *There is an altar with its lighted candles on one side,*
>> *in the rear are vaulted arches and in the back wall a*
>> *stained-glass window. Across the stage, below all this,*
>> *is a metal grille work. The singing continues)*

SOLO

> Dominus a dextris tuis,
> confregit in die irae suae reges.

RESPONSE

> De torrente in via bibet:
> propterea in exaltabit caput.

3

SOLO
> Gloria Patri, et Filio,
> et Spiritui Sancto.

RESPONSE
> Sicut erat in principio,
> et nunc, et semper,
> et in saecula saeculorum.
>   Amen.

> Rex admirabilis,
> Et triumphator nobilis,
> Dulcedo ineffabilis,
> Totus desiderabilis,
> Totus desiderabilis.

> (*During the chanting some nuns have approached the altar and knelt in prayer. Others have crossed in front of the grille, one carrying milk pails on a shoulder yoke, another a large laundry basket, three or four with musical instruments. We hear the Angelus bells. All the nuns kneel, bow their heads, cross themselves, then rise and go on about their business, as the singing changes to "Alleluia."* SISTER BERTHE *enters with a notebook and pencil. As the nuns and postulants come on from various directions and pass her she checks their names off in the book. There seems to be someone missing. The singing has stopped and now we hear the voices of nuns coming from all over the Abbey*)

VOICES (*As the lights dim out*)
> Have you seen Maria?
> Isn't Maria back yet?

Where could Maria be?
Where's Maria?
Maria!
Maria! Maria!
Maria! Maria! Maria!

Dim Out

Scene Two

A mountainside near the Abbey. In the distance we see other mountains and Austrian countryside. Downstage is a large tree.

MARIA is lying on her back at the base of the tree. Although she is dressed as a postulant, her position, with one foot high in the air and her petticoat showing, is unpostulant-like. She sits up, looks around and starts to sing.

MARIA

My day in the hills
Has come to an end I know.
A star has come out
To tell me it's time to go,
But deep in the dark-green shadows
Are voices that urge me to stay.
So I pause and I wait and I listen
For one more sound,
For one more lovely thing
That the hills might say . . .

The hills are alive
With the sound of music,
With songs they have sung
For a thousand years.
The hills fill my heart
With the sound of music—

6

THE SOUND OF MUSIC

My heart wants to sing
Every song it hears.

My heart wants to beat
Like the wings
Of the birds that rise
From the lake to the trees,
My heart wants to sigh
Like a chime that flies
From a church on a breeze,
To laugh like a brook
When it trips and falls
Over stones in its way,
To sing through the night
Like a lark who is learning to pray—

I go to the hills
When my heart is lonely,
I know I will hear
What I've heard before.
My heart will be blessed
With the sound of music
And I'll sing once more.
> (*The lights dim out and the curtains close.* SISTER SOPHIA
> *enters below the curtains and crosses the stage, carrying
> a large ring of keys*)

Dim Out

Scene Three

The office of the MOTHER ABBESS. *The sparseness of the furniture gives the sense of monastic austerity. There is a desk center, an armchair on one side, a stool on the other, a prie-dieu a short distance away. There is a door on either side of the room; on the desk, an inkstand and pen and some papers inside a portfolio. Discovered are the* MOTHER ABBESS, SISTER BERTHE *and* SISTER MARGARETTA.

MOTHER ABBESS (*Seated at the desk, sorting papers*) I think we should be pleased with our efforts. Out of twenty-eight postulants, sixteen or seventeen ready to enter the novitiate. Let's consider the doubtful ones again. There's Irmagard . . .

BERTHE Reverend Mother, there's no doubt about Irmagard —the religious life is no place for the pious.

MOTHER ABBESS You mean the pretentiously pious, Sister Berthe. There's Christina, and there's Maria.

BERTHE Well, after last night I don't think there can be any doubt in the Reverend Mother's mind about Maria.

MOTHER ABBESS I gave her permission to leave the Abbey for the day.

MARGARETTA I told you, Sister Berthe—
    (*There is a knock on the door*)

8

MOTHER ABBESS Ave!
    (SISTER SOPHIA *enters*)

SOPHIA Reverend Mother, I've brought Maria. She's waiting.

MOTHER ABBESS Sister Sophia—the Mistress of the Postulants and the Mistress of the Novices do not see eye to eye about Maria. How do you feel about her?

SOPHIA I love her very dearly. But she always seems to be in trouble, doesn't she?

BERTHE Exactly what I say! (*She sings*)
    She climbs a tree and scrapes her knee,
    Her dress has got a tear.

SOPHIA
    She waltzes on her way to Mass
    And whistles on the stair.

BERTHE
    And underneath her wimple
    She has curlers in her hair—

SOPHIA
    I've even heard her singing in the Abbey!

BERTHE
    She's always late for chapel—

SOPHIA
    But her penitence is real.

9

BERTHE

She's always late for everything
Except for every meal.
I hate to have to say it
But I very firmly feel

BERTHE *and* SOPHIA

Maria's not an asset to the Abbey.

MARGARETTA

I'd like to say a word in her behalf—

MOTHER ABBESS

Then say it, Sister Margaretta.

MARGARETTA

Maria . . . makes me . . . laugh!

SOPHIA

How do you solve a problem like Maria?

MOTHER ABBESS

How do you catch a cloud and pin it down?

MARGARETTA

How do you find a word that means Maria?

BERTHE

A flibbertijibbet!

SOPHIA

A will-o'-the-wisp!

10

MARGARETTA
A clown!

MOTHER ABBESS
Many a thing you know you'd like to tell her,
Many a thing she ought to understand,

MARGARETTA
But how do you make her stay
And listen to all you say?

MOTHER ABBESS
How do you keep a wave upon the sand?

MARGARETTA
Oh, how do you solve a problem like Maria?

MOTHER ABBESS
How do you hold a moonbeam in your hand?

MARGARETTA
When I'm with her I'm confused,
Out of focus and bemused,
And I never know exactly where I am.

BERTHE
Unpredictable as weather,
She's as flighty as a feather—

MARGARETTA (*To* BERTHE)
She's a darling!

BERTHE (*To* MARGARETTA)
    She's a demon!

MARGARETTA (*To* BERTHE)
    She's a lamb!

SOPHIA
    She'll outpester any pest,
    Drive a hornet from his nest,

BERTHE
    She could throw a whirling dervish out of whirl.

MARGARETTA
    She is gentle,
    She is wild,

SOPHIA
    She's a riddle,
    She's a child.

BERTHE
    She's a headache!

MARGARETTA
    She's an angel—

MOTHER ABBESS
    She's a girl . . .
        (*They all assume the attitude of prayer, eyes toward heaven*)

12

ALL

How do you solve a problem like Maria?
How do you catch a cloud and pin it down?
How do you find a word that means Maria?

MARGARETTA

A flibbertijibbet!

SOPHIA

A will-o'-the-wisp!

BERTHE

A clown!

ALL

Many a thing you know you'd like to tell her,
Many a thing she ought to understand,

MOTHER ABBESS

But how do you make her stay?

SOPHIA

And listen to all you say?

MARGARETTA

How do you keep a wave upon the sand?

ALL

How do you solve a problem like Maria?
How do you hold a moonbeam in your hand?
(*The song ends*)

BERTHE Reverend Mother, may I just . . .

MOTHER ABBESS Now, my children, I think I should talk *to* Maria instead of *about* her. I am grateful to you all. (*The three sisters bow and exit. The* MOTHER ABBESS *rises, studying a paper. There is a knock on the door*) Ave! (MARIA *enters, goes to the* MOTHER ABBESS, *kneels and kisses her ring*) Sit down, Maria. I want to talk to you—
(MARIA *sits on the stool*)

MARIA Yes—about last night. Reverend Mother, I was on my knees most of the night because I was late—and after you'd been so kind and given me permission to leave . . .

MOTHER ABBESS (*Sitting at her desk*) It wasn't about your being late, Maria . . .

MARIA I must have awakened half the Abbey before Sister Margaretta heard me and opened the gate.

MOTHER ABBESS Maria, very few of us were asleep. We could only think that you had lost your way—and to be lost at night on that mountain!

MARIA Reverend Mother, I couldn't be lost on that mountain. That's my mountain. I was brought up on it! It was that mountain that brought me to you.

MOTHER ABBESS Oh . . . ?

MARIA When I was a little girl I used to come down the mountain, climb a tree and look over into your garden. I'd

14

see the sisters at work, and I'd hear them sing on their way
to vespers. Many times I went back up that mountain in
the dark—singing all the way. And that brings up another
transgression—I was singing yesterday—and I was singing
without your permission.

MOTHER ABBESS Maria, it's only here in the Abbey that there
is a rule about singing.

MARIA That's the hardest rule of all for me. Sister Margaretta
is always reminding me—but too late, after I've started
singing.

MOTHER ABBESS And the day you were singing in the garden
at the top of your voice—

MARIA But, Mother, it's that kind of song.

MOTHER ABBESS I came to the window and when you saw me
you stopped.

MARIA Yes—that's been on my mind ever since it happened.

MOTHER ABBESS It's been on my mind, too. I wish you hadn't
stopped. I used to sing that song when I was a child, and
I can't quite remember— Please—
    (*She gestures to* MARIA *to sing, and* MARIA *does*)

MARIA
    Raindrops on roses and whiskers on kittens,
    Bright copper kettles and warm woolen mittens.
        (*The* MOTHER ABBESS *starts to write down the words*)

15

Brown paper packages tied up with strings—
These are a few of my favorite things.

Cream-colored ponies and crisp apple strudels,
Doorbells and sleigh bells and schnitzel with noodles,
Wild geese that fly with the moon on their wings—
These are a few of my favorite things.

Girls in white dresses with blue satin sashes,
Snowflakes that stay on my nose and eyelashes,
Silver-white winters that melt into springs—
These are a few of my favorite things.

When the dog bites,
When the bee stings,
When I'm feeling sad,
I simply remember my favorite things
And then I don't feel so bad!

MOTHER ABBESS (*Rising and singing from the words she has
written*)
Raindrops on roses and whiskers on kittens,
Bright copper kettles and warm woolen mittens,
Brown paper packages tied up with strings—
These are a few of my favorite things.
(*She hands the paper and pencil to* MARIA)
Cream-colored ponies and crisp apple strudels,
Doorbells and sleigh bells and schnitzel with noodles,
Wild geese that fly with the moon on their wings—
(MARIA *sits on the edge of the desk*)
These are a few of my favorite things.

(*The* MOTHER ABBESS *looks at* MARIA, *who jumps off the desk*)
Girls in white dresses with blue satin sashes,
Snowflakes that stay on my nose and eyelashes,
Silver-white winters that melt into springs—
These are a few of my favorite things.

When the dog bites,
When the bee stings,
When I'm feeling sad,
I simply remember my favorite things
And then I don't feel so bad!

BOTH

When the dog bites,
When the bee stings,
When I'm feeling sad,
   (*The* MOTHER ABBESS *takes* MARIA's *hand*)
I simply remember my favorite things
And then I don't feel so bad!
   (*They swing their arms together until the music ends*)

MARIA   Mother! We were both singing at the top of our voices!

MOTHER ABBESS   You're right. It's that kind of a song.

MARIA   And singing it always makes me feel better. Mother, where did you learn that song?

MOTHER ABBESS   I was brought up in the mountains myself. (*She motions* MARIA *to sit again*) Maria . . . in spite of what

you saw over the Abbey wall, you weren't prepared for the way we live, were you?
(*She herself sits*)

MARIA No, Mother, but I pray and I try.

MOTHER ABBESS Tell me, Maria, what is the most important lesson you've learned here?

MARIA To find out what is the will of God and to do it.

MOTHER ABBESS Even if it is hard to accept?

MARIA Even then.

MOTHER ABBESS (*Rising*) Maria, the dress you wore when you came to us—is that still in the robing room?

MARIA Why, no, Mother, I'm sure that's been given to the poor. Sister Margaretta said that when we enter the Abbey our worldly clothes . . . Reverend Mother, why did you ask?

MOTHER ABBESS Maria, it seems to be the will of God that you leave us.

MARIA Leave! Leave here! (*She rises*) Oh, no! Mother, please no!

MOTHER ABBESS For a while only, Maria.

MARIA Don't send me away, Mother, please. This is what I want. This is my life.

18

MOTHER ABBESS But are you ready for it? Perhaps if you go out into the world again for a time you will return to us knowing what we expect of you and that we do expect it.

MARIA I know what you expect, Mother, and I'll do it. I promise.

MOTHER ABBESS Maria.

MARIA (*Yielding*) If it is God's will. Where am I to go?

MOTHER ABBESS There's a family—a family with seven children—you like children—you're very good with them. They need a governess until September.

MARIA Until September!

MOTHER ABBESS (*Writing an address on paper*) Captain von Trapp expects you this afternoon. He's a fine man—and a brave one. He was given the Maria Teresa medal by the Emperor. It was for heroism in the Adriatic.

MARIA A Captain in the Navy! Oh, Mother, he'll be very strict.

MOTHER ABBESS You're not being sent to his battleship. (*She hands* MARIA *the address. Abbey bells are heard.* MARIA *kneels. The* MOTHER ABBESS *makes the sign of the cross on* MARIA's *forehead*) Bless you, my child.
    (*She starts out*)

MARIA Reverend Mother? Have I your permission to sing?

MOTHER ABBESS Yes, my child.

(*She exits.* MARIA *rises. She looks about the room regretfully, then starts out, singing to herself*)

MARIA

These are a few of my favorite things.

(SISTER BERTHE *enters. She gives* MARIA *a reproachful look.* MARIA *stops singing and draws herself up spunkily*)

I have been given permission to sing.

(MARIA *exits*)

Dim Out

Scene Four

A corridor in the Abbey.
MARIA *enters and sings as she crosses the stage.*

MARIA (*Singing*)
    Brown paper packages tied up with strings—
    These are a few of my favorite things.
    Girls in white dresses with blue satin sashes,
    Snowflakes that stay on my nose and eyelashes,
    Silver-white winters that melt into springs—
    These are a few of my favorite things.
       (SISTER MARGARETTA *enters from the opposite side and*
       they pass each other center stage)
    When the dog bites,
    When the bee stings,
    When I'm feeling sad,
    I simply remember my favorite things
    And then I don't feel so bad!
       (MARIA *exits*)

MARGARETTA (*Shaking her head and singing*) How do you
hold a moonbeam in your hand?
    (*She exits*)

Dim Out

Scene Five

The living room of the TRAPP *villa.*

It is a beautiful large room, two stories high, baroque in style and handsomely furnished.

Down left there is a door to the dining room, above this are two large French windows, opening on a terrace. Through these windows can be seen a mountain not too far in the distance. Between the two windows is a magnificent porcelain stove. Down right is a door to the CAPTAIN'S *library. Upstage of this door a circular stairway curves to a second-floor landing, which forms a small balcony over the back of the living room. There is an exit, right, on the balcony, presumably leading to the other rooms on this floor. On the left of the balcony we see the first few steps of a curved staircase to the third floor.*

On the ground floor, upstage under the balcony, are double doors opening on the hallway which leads to the outer door of the house, off right.

In the curve of the staircase are a small table and a side chair. Stage left there is a sofa with a single chair at its right.

A moment after the curtain has risen CAPTAIN GEORG VON TRAPP *enters on the balcony from the right. He is dressed informally and is scanning a letter which he is holding in his hand. He stops at the railing of the balcony, takes a silver boatswain's whistle from his pocket, and blows a distinctive signal on it. He waits a few seconds, and as no one answers he repeats the signal. Then he starts down the stairs. Halfway down, seeing no one has appeared, he blows a different signal.*

22

Almost immediately, FRANZ, *the butler, enters from the dining room. He is a man of middle-age who was previously the* CAPTAIN'S *orderly in the Imperial Navy. He is dressed in a butler's working apron, is wearing gloves and is carrying a metal tray and a polishing cloth.*

FRANZ   Yes, sir?

CAPTAIN   I was calling the housekeeper and she didn't answer. Do you know why?

FRANZ   Sometimes she doesn't hear, sir.

FRAU SCHMIDT   (*Entering from the dining room*)   I'm sorry, sir, I was answering the telephone. Good day, sir. We're happy to have you home again.

CAPTAIN   Why did the last governess leave?

FRAU SCHMIDT   Who knows? She just said, "I've had enough of this," and walked out.

CAPTAIN   Why? Was Louisa playing tricks again?— Putting toads in her bed?

FRAU SCHMIDT   She didn't complain of that, sir.

CAPTAIN   Well, there's another one coming today. And this one can't walk out.

FRAU SCHMIDT   Oh?

CAPTAIN She's coming from Nonnberg Abbey with orders to stay until September.

FRAU SCHMIDT I hope you'll be at home for a time, sir.

CAPTAIN Just until tomorrow. The telephone call—was it for me?

FRAU SCHMIDT No, sir, it was for Franz. Before you arrived there was a call from Vienna—a Frau Schraeder. I have the number in the pantry.

CAPTAIN (*Starting out*) I know the number. Oh, I shall be back in about a month with some guests.

FRAU SCHMIDT Yes, sir. Do you know how many, sir?

CAPTAIN Just two. Herr Detweiler—

FRANZ Ah, Herr Detweiler.

CAPTAIN And Frau Schraeder.
(*He exits into the library*)

FRANZ Who wanted me on the telephone?

FRAU SCHMIDT It was the post office. They've got a telegram for you. It will be delivered at seven o'clock.

FRANZ Seven o'clock? That gives me five hours to be nervous.

FRAU SCHMIDT (*Going upstairs*) With that scatterbrained boy delivering telegrams—

24

FRANZ Well, that's one thing people are saying—if the Germans did take over Austria, we'd have efficiency.

FRAU SCHMIDT Don't let the Captain hear you say that. (*The* CAPTAIN *whistles offstage*) He didn't whistle for us when his wife was alive.

FRANZ He's being the captain of a ship again.
(*The* CAPTAIN *whistles again*)

FRAU SCHMIDT I can't bear being whistled for—it's humiliating.

FRANZ In the Imperial Navy, the bosun always whistled for us.
(*We hear the doorbell*)

FRAU SCHMIDT But I wasn't in the Imperial Navy.

FRANZ Too bad. You could have made a fortune. (*He exits into the hallway toward the outer door.* FRAU SCHMIDT *comes down the stairs and exits into the library.* FRANZ *re-enters, followed by* MARIA) You will wait here.
(*He exits into the library.* MARIA *is wearing a dress that has been designed by an enemy of the female sex, and an unbecoming hat. She is carrying a small carpetbag and a guitar in its case. She comes down into the room timidly and looks around in awe at the handsome embellishments. She puts the guitar case down on the floor and starts toward the windows, touching the porcelain stove admiringly as she passes it. In the distance we hear the Abbey bells. She kneels and bows her head in*

25

a brief prayer. The CAPTAIN *enters from the library, the letter still in his hand. As he sees* MARIA *in prayer, he stops.* MARIA *crosses herself and rises)*

CAPTAIN I'm Captain von Trapp. You are Fraulein . . .

MARIA Maria—Maria Rainer.

CAPTAIN Now, Fraulein, as to your duties here—(*He suddenly becomes aware of her dress*) Would you mind stepping over there? (*He indicates a spot in the center of the room.* MARIA *slowly moves to it*) Before the children meet you, you will put on another dress.

MARIA I haven't any other dress. When we enter the Abbey our worldly clothes are given to the poor.

CAPTAIN What about this one?

MARIA The poor didn't want this one.

CAPTAIN This is what you would call a worldly dress?

MARIA It belonged to our last postulant. I would have made myself a dress but I wasn't given time. I can make my own clothes.

CAPTAIN Good. I'll see that you're given some material—today if possible. Now, you will be in charge of my children. There are seven of them. You will find out how far they have progressed in their studies and carry on from there. Each morning will be spent in the classroom. Each after-

noon, they march along the paths of the estate. You will see
that at all times they conduct themselves with decorum and
orderliness. The first rule in this house is discipline.

MARIA   Yes, sir.

(*The* CAPTAIN *takes out his silver whistle and blows a
siren-like summoning blast which continues while his
children enter from both sides of the balcony, the outside door, the French windows and the library, and
end by forming a single line with* GRETL *and* MARTA *on
the stairs,* KURT, LOUISA, FRIEDRICH *and* LIESL, *in that
order, on the balcony behind them. They are dressed
in white sailor uniforms; the girls, of course, in white
skirts. The* CAPTAIN *changes his signal to one that marks
time for marching, and, led by* GRETL, *they march down
the stairs and, with a military left turn at the foot of the
stairs, line up across the stage.* MARIA *has watched this
with considerable astonishment. There is an empty
space between* MARTA *and* KURT. *Slowly through the
dining-room door,* BRIGITTA *enters, reading a book. The*
CAPTAIN *sees her, takes the book away from her, puts it
on the sofa, and gives her an admonishing pat on the
behind, which sends her running to take her place in
formation. The* CAPTAIN *crosses in front of them to the
other side of* LIESL *and addresses them*)

CAPTAIN   This is your new fraulein—Fraulein Maria. As I
sound your signal you will step forward and repeat your
name. You, Fraulein, will listen and learn their signals so
that you can call them when you want them. (*He whistles
their various signals. Each child responds to his or her signal, stepping forward in a military manner, announcing*

27

his or her name, then stepping back into line. The CAPTAIN
crosses below the children to MARIA, *taking from his pocket
a velvet case which holds another boatswain's whistle. He
hands it to* MARIA) Now, Fraulein, let's see how well you
listened.

(MARIA, *slightly bewildered, takes the whistle from its
case*)

MARIA I won't have to whistle for them, Reverend Captain—
What I mean is, I'll be with them all the time.

CAPTAIN Not on all occasions. This is a large house and a
large estate. They have been taught to come only when they
hear their signal. Now when I want you, this is what you'll
hear.

(*The* CAPTAIN *whistles the governess' signal*)

MARIA You won't have to trouble, sir, because I couldn't answer to a whistle.

CAPTAIN That's nonsense. Everyone in this house answers to
a whistle. I'll show you.

(*He whistles the butler's signal*)

FRANZ (*Entering and coming to attention*) Yes, sir?

CAPTAIN This is my orderly—my butler. The new governess
—Fraulein Maria.

(*He whistles the housekeeper's signal*)

FRAU SCHMIDT (*Entering on the balcony*) Yes, sir?

28

CAPTAIN That is the executive officer, Frau Schmidt, the housekeeper. Fraulein Maria. Please be sure that her room is ready.

FRAU SCHMIDT Yes, sir.
  (FRANZ *takes* MARIA's *bag from her and goes upstairs to the balcony*)

CAPTAIN Well, I shall now leave you with the children. You are in command.
  (*He starts out.* MARIA *blows a blast on the whistle. He stops and turns*)

MARIA Pardon me, sir—I don't know how to address you.

CAPTAIN You will call me Captain.

MARIA (*Going to the* CAPTAIN) Thank you, Captain. I forgot to return this whistle, Captain. I won't need it, Captain. (*He takes the whistle, stares at her a moment, then exits. Children snap to attention.* FRANZ *and* FRAU SCHMIDT *exit to the third floor*) Well, now that there's just us, would you tell me your names again, and tell me how old you are.
  (*Each child, in turn, steps forward in military manner*)

LIESL I'm Liesl. I'm sixteen years old and I don't need a governess.

MARIA I'm glad you told me. We'll just be friends.

FRIEDRICH I'm Friedrich. I'm fourteen. I'm a boy.

MARIA Boy? Why, you're almost a man.
(FRIEDRICH *looks pleased.* LOUISA *signals the other girls, who giggle*)

LOUISA I'm Brigitta.

MARIA (*Crossing behind* LOUISA *and pulling up her braid*) You didn't tell me how old you are, Louisa.

BRIGITTA (*Stepping forward*) *I'm* Brigitta. She's Louisa and she's thirteen years old and you're smart. I'm nine and I think your dress is the ugliest one I ever saw.

KURT Brigitta, you mustn't say a thing like that.

BRIGITTA Why not? Don't you think it's ugly?

KURT If I did think so, I wouldn't say so. I'm Kurt, I'm eleven—almost.

MARIA That's a nice age to be, eleven—almost.

MARTA (*Pulling* MARIA's *skirt*) I'm Marta and I'm going to be seven on Tuesday and I'd like a pink parasol.

MARIA Pink is my favorite color, too. (GRETL *steps forward*) And you're Gretl. (GRETL *smiles*) I'm going to tell you something. (MARIA *sits*) I've never been a governess before. How do I start?

LOUISA You mean you don't know anything about being a governess?

MARIA No.

LOUISA Well, the first thing you have to do is to tell Father to mind his own business.

KURT No, Louisa, don't. I like her.

BRIGITTA (*Picking up the guitar case*) What's in here?

MARIA My guitar.

BRIGITTA What did you bring this for?

MARIA For when we all sing together.

MARTA (BRIGITTA *takes the guitar out of the case*) We don't sing.

MARIA Of course you sing. Everybody sings. What songs do you know?

KURT We don't know any songs.

MARIA (*Taking the guitar from* BRIGITTA) You don't?

ALL No.

MARIA Well . . . Now I know where to start. I'm going to teach you how to sing. (*She plays the guitar and sings*)
Let's start at the very beginning
A very good place to start.
When you read you begin with—

GRETL
A, B, C.

MARIA
When you sing you begin with do re mi.

CHILDREN
Do re mi?

MARIA
Do re mi.
The first three notes just happen to be
Do re mi.

CHILDREN
Do re mi!

MARIA
Do re mi fa so la ti—
    (*Speaking*)
Come, I'll make it easier. Listen. (*Singing*)
    Doe—a deer, a female deer,
    Ray—a drop of golden sun,
    Me—a name I call myself,
    Far—a long, long way to run,
    Sew—a needle pulling thread,
    La—a note to follow sew,
    Tea—a drink with jam and bread.
    That will bring us back to do-oh-oh-oh!

GRETL
Doe—

MARIA
A deer, a female deer,

CHILDREN
Ray—

MARIA
A drop of golden sun,
Me—a name I call myself,
Far—a long, long way to run,
Sew—

ALL
A needle pulling thread,
La—a note to follow sew,
Tea—a drink with jam and bread.

MARIA
That will bring us back to—

CHILDREN
Doe—a deer, a female deer,
Ray—a drop of golden sun,
Me—a name I call myself,
Far—a long, long way to run,
Sew—a needle pulling thread,
La—a note to follow sew,
Tea—a drink with jam and bread.

MARIA
That will bring us back to do.
Do re mi fa so la ti do.

CHILDREN
So do!

BRIGITTA (*Speaking*) Is that what you call a song? Do re mi fa so and so on?

MARIA No. Do re mi fa so and so on are only the tools we use to build a song. Once we have these notes in our heads we can sing a million different tunes.

FRIEDRICH How?

MARIA By mixing them up. Listen. (*Singing*)
So do la fa mi do re.
(*Speaking*)
Now you do it.

CHILDREN
So do la fa mi do re.

MARIA
So do la ti do re do.

CHILDREN
So do la ti do re do!

MARIA (*Speaking*) Now, let's put it all together—

CHILDREN
So do la fa mi do re
So do la ti do re do!

BRIGITTA (*Speaking*) But it doesn't mean anything.

34

MARIA (*Speaking*) So we put in words—one word for every
note. (*Singing*)
   When you know the notes to sing
   You can sing most anything.

BRIGITTA (*Speaking*) You said one word for every note.

MARIA Yes, Brigitta, I did.

BRIGITTA But when you sing—(*Singing*)
   "anything"
   (*Speaking*)—you are using up three notes on one word.

MARIA Yes. That's right. Well, sometimes we do that. Now,
altogether.
   (*She hands the guitar to* BRIGITTA, *who puts it behind
   the sofa*)

ALL (*Singing*)
   When you know the notes to sing
   You can sing most anything.

GRETL (MARIA *leads her across the room*)
   Doe—

ALL
   A deer, a female deer,

MARTA (*Marches to join* GRETL)
   Ray—

ALL
   A drop of golden sun,

35

BRIGITTA (*Curtsies to* MARIA *and joins the first two*)
Me—

ALL
A name I call myself,

KURT (*Shakes* MARIA's *hand and crosses*)
Far—

ALL
A long, long way to run,

LOUISA (MARIA *holds her pigtail as she crosses*)
Sew—

ALL
A needle pulling thread,

FRIEDRICH (*Bows to* MARIA *and crosses*)
La—

ALL
A note to follow sew,

LIESL (*Joining the others*)
Tea—

ALL
A drink with jam and bread.
That will bring us back to do.

CHILDREN (*Carillon effect as* MARIA *taps each one on the top of the head*)

36

Do re mi fa so la ti do do
Ti la so fa mi re
Do mi mi
Mi so so
Re fa fa
La ti ti
Do mi mi
Mi so so
Re fa fa
La ti ti

MARIA

When you know the notes to sing
You can sing most anything.

ALL (*Led by* MARIA, *all march around the room and back to the sofa, where the children group around her*)
Doe—a deer, a female deer,
Ray—a drop of golden sun,
Me—a name I call myself,
Far—a long, long way to run,
Sew—a needle pulling thread—

CHILDREN
A needle pulling thread,

MARIA
La—a note to follow sew—

CHILDREN
A note to follow sew,

37

MARIA
    Tea—a drink with jam and bread—

CHILDREN
    Jam and bread.

MARIA (*Rising*)
    That will bring us back to do.

ALL (*The children crowd around* MARIA)
    That will bring us back to—

MARIA (*Going down the scale until her final "do" is practically bass*)
    Do ti la so fa mi re do

ALL (*Shouting*)
    Do!

Blackout

Scene Six

Outside the villa. We see the villa and a wall that runs around it. At left is a stone bench.

After a moment LIESL *enters, turns and waves to someone offstage.*

LIESL Good night, Rolf.

ROLF (*Walking on with his bicycle*) Liesl!

LIESL (*Going to him*) Yes?

ROLF You don't have to say good night this early just because your father's home—

LIESL How did you know my father was home?

ROLF Oh, I have a way of knowing things.

LIESL You're wonderful.

ROLF (*Resting the bicycle on its stand*) Oh, no, I'm not—really.

LIESL Oh, yes you are. I mean—how did you know two days ago that you would be here at just this time tonight with a telegram for Franz?

39

ROLF Every year on this date he always gets a birthday telegram from his sister.

LIESL You see—you *are* wonderful.

ROLF Can I come again tomorrow night?

LIESL (*Sitting on the bench*) Rolf, you can't be sure you're going to have a telegram to deliver here tomorrow night.

ROLF (*Sitting beside her*) I could come here by mistake—with a telegram for Colonel Schneider. He's here from Berlin. He's staying with the Gauleiter but I—(*Suddenly concerned*) No one's supposed to know he's here. Don't you tell your father.

LIESL Why not?

ROLF Well, your father's pretty Austrian.

LIESL We're all Austrian.

ROLF Some people think we ought to be German. They're pretty mad at those who don't think so. They're getting ready to—well, let's hope your father doesn't get into any trouble.
(*He goes to his bicycle*)

LIESL (*Rising*) Don't worry about Father. He was decorated for bravery.

ROLF I know. I don't worry about him. The only one I worry about is his daughter.

LIESL (*Standing behind the bench*) Me? Why?
    (ROLF *gestures to her to stand on the bench. She does and he studies her*)

ROLF How old are you, Liesl?

LIESL Sixteen— What's wrong with that?
    (*He answers in song*)

ROLF (*Singing*)
    You wait, little girl, on an empty stage
    For fate to turn the light on,
    Your life, little girl, is an empty page
    That men will want to write on—

LIESL
    To write on.

ROLF
    You are sixteen, going on seventeen,
    Baby, it's time to think.
    Better beware,
    Be canny and careful,
    Baby, you're on the brink.

    You are sixteen, going on seventeen,
    Fellows will fall in line,
    Eager young lads
    And roués and cads
    Will offer you food and wine.

Totally unprepared are you
To face a world of men,
Timid and shy and scared are you
Of things beyond your ken.

You need someone older and wiser
Telling you what to do . . .
I am seventeen, going on eighteen,
I'll take care of you.
    (LIESL *dances. At the end of the dance* ROLF *gets on his bicycle as if to leave;* LIESL *hurries to him*)

LIESL (*Singing*)
    I am sixteen, going on seventeen,
    I know that I'm naïve.
    Fellows I meet
    May tell me I'm sweet
    And willingly I'll believe.

    I am sixteen, going on seventeen,
    Innocent as a rose.
    Bachelor dandies,
    Drinkers of brandies—
    What do I know of those?

    Totally unprepared am I
    To face a world of men,
    Timid and shy and scared am I
    Of things beyond my ken.

    I need someone older and wiser
    Telling me what to do . . .

Mary Martin and Theodore Bikel, as MARIA and the CAPTAIN

THE SOUND OF MUSIC

You are seventeen, going on eighteen,
I'll depend on you.

> (LIESL *dances again.* ROLF *gets off his bicycle to watch
> her. At the end of the dance she puts her arms around
> him. They kiss, break away in confusion, and* ROLF
> *jumps on his bicycle and rides off.* LIESL *shouts with
> joy and runs off in the opposite direction*)

Blackout

Scene Seven

MARIA's *bedroom. The gabled ceiling suggests it is on the top floor of the villa. The door from the hallway is in the upstage wall. At the left of this door is a wardrobe with double doors. The left wall slants away from this, and in it is a window. To the right of the door to the hall is an alcove, curtained off with drapes of yellow and brown cretonne, matching the drapes of the window. Below the alcove, in a jog, is* MARIA's *double brass bed with a thick eiderdown comforter.*

FRAU SCHMIDT (*Off*) Fraulein Maria! (*She enters carrying a bolt of cloth*) Fraulein Maria, it's Frau Schmidt.

MARIA (*Off*) I'm getting ready for bed.

FRAU SCHMIDT The Captain is going to Vienna tomorrow. I have this material he ordered for a new dress for you.

MARIA (*Off*) Oh, how nice of him. (*She enters from the alcove, wearing a nightgown under a dressing robe.* FRAU SCHMIDT *hands her the bolt of material*) Even before it's made, this is the prettiest dress I've ever had. I hope the Captain will like it, because I want to ask him for more material.

FRAU SCHMIDT More?

44

MARIA Oh, not for me—for the children. For play clothes. (*She takes the material into the alcove*)

FRAU SCHMIDT (*Crossing to the window and closing the curtains*) The Von Trapp children never play. The Captain doesn't like them to get dirty.

MARIA (*Re-entering*) But they're children. They have to climb trees, roll on the grass. Think of all the rocks and caves—

FRAU SCHMIDT The Captain says the best exercise is marching. The children will continue to march. I hope you find your room comfortable.

MARIA Yes, thank you.

FRAU SCHMIDT (*Going to the bed and adjusting the eiderdown comforter*) There will be new curtains for the window and the alcove. They will be hung tomorrow.

MARIA (*At the window*) But these curtains are very good.

FRAU SCHMIDT There will be new curtains.

MARIA (*Measuring the drapes at arm's length from her nose*) Will the Captain be away long?

FRAU SCHMIDT I don't know. Of course he has to come home every time he hires a new governess. I sometimes think the children get rid of their governesses just because they want to see their father.

THE SOUND OF MUSIC

MARIA (*Picking up her guitar case*) He must want to see them, too.

FRAU SCHMIDT Since his wife died, they remind him too much of her. (*Seeing the guitar*) You can put that away. You won't be using it.

MARIA Why not?

FRAU SCHMIDT The Captain won't have music here.

MARIA He won't have music???

FRAU SCHMIDT And he used to love music. There were wonderful evenings here. His wife would sing and he would play the violin or guitar. But now he's shut all that out of his life.

MARIA So that's why he's the way he is. But not to have music—that's wrong for him and wrong for the children, too.
    (*She puts the guitar in the alcove*)

FRAU SCHMIDT It will work out. The Captain may marry again before the summer is over.

MARIA (*Re-entering*) That would change everything. They'd have a mother again.

FRAU SCHMIDT (*Dismissingly*) It's going to rain. You'd better close your window.
    (*She exits.* MARIA *goes to the bed and kneels in prayer*)

MARIA Dear God, I know now that You have sent me here on a mission. I must help these children to love their new mother and prepare them to win her love so she will never want them to leave her. And I pray that this will become a happy family in Thy sight. God bless the Captain, God bless Liesl, and Friedrich, Louisa, Brigitta, Marta, and little Gretl—and, oh, yes, I forgot the other boy—what's his name? Well, God bless what's-his-name! (*There is a flash of lightning.* LIESL *enters through the window. Her dress is smudged with dirt. She tiptoes to the hall door.* MARIA *sees her out of the corner of her eye, but continues*) God bless the Reverend Mother, and Sister Margaretta and everybody at Nonnberg Abbey. And now, dear God, about Liesl— (LIESL *stops and gives* MARIA *a startled look*) Help her to know that I am her friend and help her to tell me what she's up to.

LIESL Are you going to tell on me?

MARIA (*Silencing her with a gesture*) Help me to be understanding so that I may guide her footsteps. In the name of the Father, and of the Son, and of the Holy Ghost. Amen. (MARIA *rises*)

LIESL I was out taking a walk and somebody locked the doors earlier than usual—and I didn't want to wake everybody up —so when I saw your window open— You're not going to tell Father, are you?

MARIA (*Looking out the window*) Did you climb that trellis to get up here?

THE SOUND OF MUSIC

LIESL That's how we always got into this room to play tricks on the governess. (*Proudly*) Louisa can climb it with a toad in her hand.

MARIA Liesl, were you out walking all by yourself? (LIESL *shakes her head negatively*) You know, if we wash that dress out tonight, nobody would notice it tomorrow. Then all this would be just between you and me. You could put this on—(*She takes off her robe and puts it around* LIESL's *shoulders*) Take your dress in there—and put it to soak in the bathtub. (*Thunder and lightning. They embrace each other in fright*) Then come back here and sit on the edge of my bed and we'll have a talk.

LIESL I told you today I didn't need a governess. Well, maybe I do.
          (*She exits into the alcove. Lightning and thunder.* MARIA *jumps, then crosses to the bed and peers under the comforter, looking for possible toads.* GRETL *enters in her nightdress*)

MARIA Oh, it's you, Gretl. Are you afraid? (GRETL *shakes her head. Thunder and lightning.* GRETL *jumps up on the bed with* MARIA) You're not afraid of a thunderstorm, are you? You just stay right here with me. Where are the others?

GRETL They're asleep. They're not scared.
          (*Thunder and lightning.* BRIGITTA *and* LOUISA *run on in their nightdresses,* MARTA *trailing after them*)

MARTA Wait for me.
48

MARIA (*To* GRETL) Oh, no? Look. (*To the others*) Come, all of you. Up on the bed. (*The three girls jump up on the bed*) Now all we have to do is wait for the boys.

LOUISA We won't see them! Boys are brave.
  (*Thunder and lightning.* KURT *and* FRIEDRICH *enter in their pajamas*)

MARIA You boys aren't frightened, too, are you?

KURT Oh, no. We just wanted to be sure you weren't.

MARIA Was this your idea, Friedrich?

FRIEDRICH Oh, no. It was Kurt's.

MARIA That's it, Kurt. That's the one I left out. (*Looking up*) God bless Kurt.
  (*Lightning and thunder. The boys run and cower at the foot of the bed*)

MARTA Why does it do that?

MARIA Well, the lightning says something to the thunder and the thunder answers it back.

MARTA I wish it wouldn't answer so loud.

MARIA Maybe if we all sing loud enough we won't hear the thunder. (*The children climb off the bed and sit in a semi-circle at its foot.* MARIA *sings*)
  High on a hill was a lonely goatherd,
    Layee odl, layee odl layee o

Loud was the voice of the lonely goatherd,
  Layee odl layee odl o

Folks in a town that was quite remote, heard
  Layee odl layee odl layee o
Lusty and clear from the goatherd's throat, heard
  Layee odl layee odl o
  O ho lay-dee odl lee o
  O ho lay-dee odl ay!
  O ho lay-dee odl lee o
  Hodl odl lee-o-lay!

A prince on the bridge of a castle moat, heard
  Layee odl, layee odl layee o
Men on a road with a load to tote, heard
  Layee odl layee odl o
Men in the midst of a table d'hôte, heard
  Layee odl layee odl layee ee o
Men drinking beer with the foam afloat, heard
  O ho lay-dee odl lee o
  O ho lay-dee odl ay!
  O ho lay-dee odl lee o
    (*Lightning and thunder*)
  Hodl odl lee-o-lay!
    (GRETL *jumps on the bed*)
One little girl in a pale pink coat, heard
  Layee odl, layee odl layee o
She yodeled back to the lonely goatherd,
  Layee odl layee odl o

Soon her Mama with a gleaming gloat, heard
   Layee odl layee odl layee o
What a duet for a girl and goatherd!
   Layee odl layee odl o
    (*The other girls jump on the bed*)
   O ho lay-dee odl lee o
   O ho lay-dee odl ay!
   O ho lay-dee odl lee o
   Hodl odl lee-o-lay!

Happy are they—lay lee o layee lee o
   O lay lee o lay lee lay ee o
Soon the duet will become a trio!
   Layee odl layee odl o
   Hodi lay-ee

LIESL (*Sticking her head out of the alcove*)
   Hodi lay-ee

MARIA
   Hodi lay-ee
    (GRETL *pulls* LIESL *into the room*)

LIESL
   Hodi lay-ee

MARIA
   Hodi lay-ee

LIESL
   Hodi lay-ee

MARIA
O-de-layee odl lee-ee odl lay!
(*There is a very loud crash of thunder and a flash of lightning.* MARIA *and the children jump on the bed and huddle together*)

Blackout

Scene Eight

A hallway in the TRAPP *villa.*

GRETL *enters carrying a lighted candle, followed by* MARTA, BRIGITTA *and* LOUISA. LOUISA *has hold of* GRETL'S *nightdress;* BRIGITTA *holds* LOUISA'S, *and* MARTA, BRIGITTA'S. *There is a crash of thunder. They hesitate, then go on, and* GRETL *starts to yodel bravely, but tremulously. There is another crash of thunder.* MARTA, LOUISA *and* BRIGITTA *turn around and run off.* GRETL, *who is not aware of this, continues, then senses something is wrong. She reaches behind her for the others, turns and sees she is alone. There is a clap of thunder. She runs off.*

Blackout

Scene Nine

The terrace of the TRAPP *villa.*

The villa is stage right. Since the terrace is off the living room, people entering from the house come through the French windows of the living room. Over these windows is a striped awning. Convenient to these windows are a terrace table and two chairs. On the table is a tray with coffee service. From the upstage end of the villa a short balustrade extends toward stage left, a potted plant on its terminal post. There is an exit toward the gardens on stage left between this balustrade and a boxwood hedge on the left side of the terrace. In front of this hedge is a garden bench and a stool. The view the audience sees beyond the villa is of the Alps.

FRANZ *is standing behind the table, pouring coffee.* ELSA SCHRAEDER, *a handsome woman in her late thirties, cosmopolitan, alert and attractive, is seated left of the table, admiring the view of other mountains somewhere beyond the audience.* CAPTAIN VON TRAPP *is standing center, admiring* ELSA.

CAPTAIN Franz, did you tell Herr Detweiler we're having coffee out here?

FRANZ Yes, sir. Herr Detweiler is still on the telephone.
     (URSULA *enters from the house with a tray of pastry*)

URSULA (*Offering tray*) Frau Schraeder?

ELSA Oh, thank you.
     (*She takes a pastry.* URSULA *exits into the house*)

54

CAPTAIN No sign of the children, Franz?

FRANZ Not yet, sir.
(FRANZ *exits into the house*)

ELSA (*Rising*) Georg, those mountains—they're magnificent!

CAPTAIN Yes, they're not like any other mountains—they're friendly. Look, that green stretch of woods over there—when the wind moves through it, it's like a restless sea.

ELSA And that sweet little village.

CAPTAIN (*With mock sternness*) That's not a village. That's a town.

ELSA Oh, I'm sorry—I didn't mean to hurt its feelings.
(*She returns to her chair*)

CAPTAIN It's fun being with you. You're quite an experience for me.

ELSA You're quite an experience for me, too. Somewhere in you there's a fascinating man. Occasionally I catch a glimpse of him, and when I do, he's exciting.

CAPTAIN Exciting? I've never been called exciting before.

ELSA I'm beginning to understand you better now that I see you here— You know, you're a little like those mountains—except that you keep moving. How can you be away from this place as much as you are?

55

CAPTAIN Maybe I've been searching for a reason to come back here to stay.

ELSA (*Pointedly*) Georg, I like it here very much.

CAPTAIN (*Avoiding the point*) Max can't still be on the telephone. I know he's desperate about getting singers for the Kaltzberg Festival but—(*To* ELSA) You like it here?

ELSA Oh, we'd have to spend some time in Vienna, I have Heinrich's estate to look after.

CAPTAIN I thought that was a corporation now.

ELSA It is and I'm president.

CAPTAIN You president of a corporation!

ELSA After all, I managed Heinrich's affairs for years before he died.

CAPTAIN I can't see you sitting behind a desk.

ELSA Well, of course, I wear a business suit and smoke a big cigar.
(FRANZ *enters from the house*)

FRANZ Excuse me, Captain, Herr Detweiler would like his coffee.

CAPTAIN While he's telephoning?

56

FRANZ   Yes, sir.
  (FRANZ *pours a cup of coffee.* MAX DETWEILER *enters. He
  is a charming dilettante. He carries a small notebook
  and a pencil*)

MAX   I'm sorry I took so long.

CAPTAIN   Any luck?

MAX   How would you like this for the Kaltzberg Festival—
  the finest choral group in Austria, the greatest mixed quartet
  in all Europe—and the best soprano in the world?

ELSA   Max, that's something I'd love to hear!

MAX   So would I. All I've got up to now is a basso who isn't
  even profundo.
  (FRANZ *exits into the house*)

ELSA   Max, you always come up with a good Festival Concert.
  (MAX *sits on a garden stool. The* CAPTAIN *takes him a
  cup of coffee with a piece of pastry on the saucer*)

MAX   And why? Because my motto is: "Never start out looking for the people you wind up getting." That's why I've
  been telephoning Paris, Rome, Stockholm, London—

ELSA   On Georg's telephone?

MAX   How else could I afford it? Why am I up here?

CAPTAIN   I hoped it was because you liked me.

MAX Of course I like you. Why shouldn't I like you? You live like a king. You have an excellent wine cellar—

ELSA Max!

MAX I like rich people. I like the way they live. I like the way *I* live when I'm with them. (*We hear the Abbey bells*) Georg, speaking as a government official, I—Georg, is there a cathedral around here?

CAPTAIN That's our Abbey—Nonnberg Abbey.

MAX Do they have a choir?

CAPTAIN I think so.

MAX Good! In the next few days I have to visit all these towns around here and listen to *saengerbünde,* choirs, quartets—

CAPTAIN You'll be here for meals, won't you?

MAX Oh, yes! (MAX *rises and looks off over the heads of the audience, where* MAX *plainly sees a mountain village*) It was in a town just about that size—Watzmann—where I discovered the St. Ignatius Boys Choir. In nineteen thirty they won the Festival, became very famous, toured all over the world.

ELSA Oh, yes—whatever became of them?

MAX By the time their voices changed they were rich enough to live in America. (*Indicating*) Who lives in that dilapidated castle down there? Rumpelstiltskin?

58

CAPTAIN Baron Elberfeld. The oldest family in the valley.

ELSA I'd like to meet him. I'd like to meet all your friends here. Georg, why don't you give a dinner for me while I'm here? Nothing very much—just something lavish.

CAPTAIN I wouldn't know whom to invite. Today it's difficult to tell who's a friend and who's an enemy.

ELSA This isn't a good time to make enemies. Let's make some friends.
(*Wishing to change the subject, the* CAPTAIN *goes upstage and looks off*)

CAPTAIN I can't understand what's happened to the children.

ELSA You're not worried about them, are you?

CAPTAIN They should have been here to welcome you.

ELSA It couldn't have been an intentional slight, because they haven't met me yet.

CAPTAIN Forgive me, I'll try to find them.
(*He exits*)

MAX Elsa, have you made up Georg's mind yet? Is he going to marry you?

ELSA Oh, yes! Of course, he hasn't admitted it yet. There seems to be something standing in his way.

MAX You don't know what it is?

ELSA No.

MAX I do.

ELSA What?

MAX It's very simple. It's money.

ELSA Money?

MAX Yes. He's rich and you're rich. (*He sings*)

In all the famous love affairs
The lovers have to struggle.
In garret rooms away upstairs
The lovers starve and snuggle.
They're famous for misfortune which
They seem to have no fear of,
While lovers who are very rich
You very seldom hear of.
    (*The* CAPTAIN *enters and comes down to them*)

CAPTAIN (*Speaking*) Not a sign of them anywhere . . .
    (MAX *pushes* ELSA *toward the* CAPTAIN)

ELSA (*Singing to the* CAPTAIN)
    No little shack do you share with me,
    We do not flee from a mortgagee,
    Nary a care in the world have we—

MAX (*Singing*)
    How can love survive?

ELSA

    You're fond of bonds and you own a lot,
    I have a plane and a Diesel yacht,

MAX

    Plenty of nothing you haven't got!

MAX *and* ELSA

    How can love survive?

ELSA

    No rides for us
    On the top of a bus
    In the face of the freezing breezes—

MAX

    You reach your goals
      (*To the* CAPTAIN)
    In your comfy old Rolls
      (*To* ELSA)
    Or in one of your Mercedeses!

ELSA

    Far, very far off the beam are we,
    Quaint and bizarre as a team are we,
    Two millionaires with a dream are we,
    We're keeping romance alive,
    Two millionaires with a dream are we—
    We'll make our love survive . . .

    No little cold water flat have we,
    Warmed by the glow of insolvency—

MAX

> Up to your necks in security,
> How can love survive?

ELSA

> How can I show what I feel for you?
> I cannot go out and steal for you,
> I cannot die like Camille for you—
> How can love survive?

MAX

> You millionaires
> With financial affairs
> Are too busy for simple pleasure.
> When you are poor
> It is *toujours l'amour*—
> For *l'amour* all the poor have leisure!

ELSA (*To the* CAPTAIN)

> Caught in our gold-plated chains are we,
> Lost in our wealthy domains are we,
> Trapped by our capital gains are we,
> But we'll keep romance alive—
>> (MAX *turns out his empty trousers pockets*)

MAX

> Trapped by our capital gains are we—

ELSA

> We'll make our love survive!
>> (*At the end of the number* ROLF *enters, looking for* LIESL. *He is concentrating on the upstairs windows of the villa so completely, he doesn't see the others*)

CAPTAIN (*To* ROLF) What do you want?

ROLF (*Startled*) Oh, Captain . . . I didn't see, I mean, I didn't know . . . er, uh, . . . Heil!
  (*He holds his hand up in salute*)

CAPTAIN (*Icily*) Who are you?

ROLF I have a telegram for Herr Detweiler.

MAX (*Taking the telegram from* ROLF) I am Herr Detweiler.

CAPTAIN You've delivered your telegram, now get out!
  (ROLF *exits, flustered*)

ELSA Georg, he's just a boy!

CAPTAIN I am an Austrian—I will not be heiled!

MAX Georg, why don't you look at things the way I do? What's going to happen is going to happen. Just be sure it doesn't happen to you.
  (ELSA *exits into the house*)

CAPTAIN Max, it's a good thing you haven't any character, because if you had I'm convinced I'd hate you.

MAX You couldn't hate me. I'm too lovable.
  (FRANZ *enters from the house*)

FRANZ Herr Detweiler, there's a call for you. It's from—

MAX (*Quickly*) I'll take it.

(MAX *exits into the house, followed by* FRANZ. *At this moment the* CAPTAIN'S *attention is attracted by the sound of voices yodeling and coming from the direction of the garden.* GRETL *runs on and stoops over. Next we see* MARTA *leapfrog over* GRETL *and stoop. She is followed by* BRIGITTA, KURT, LOUISA, FRIEDRICH *and* LIESL, *all leapfrogging. They are dressed in play clothes made from the curtains we have seen in* MARIA'S *bedroom. The last one on, yodeling along with the children, dressed in a dirndl made from the material the* CAPTAIN *sent her, is* MARIA. *Her leapfrogging takes her to the feet of the* CAPTAIN. *She straightens up in pleased surprise*)

MARIA Oh, Captain—you're home!

CHILDREN (*Joyfully*) Father! Father, you're home!
(*The* CAPTAIN *takes his whistle from his pocket and blows a peremptory blast. The children, dismayed, line up in military fashion*)

CAPTAIN Straight line! (*The* CAPTAIN *crosses behind them, inspecting their strange garb with evident displeasure. He takes from* LOUISA'S *head a kerchief made of the curtain material*) Get cleaned up! Get into your uniforms and report back here! (*The children glance appealingly toward* MARIA) At once! (*The children run into the house*) Fraulein! Where did they get these abominations—out of a nightmare?

MARIA No, out of the curtains—the curtains that used to hang in my bedroom. There was plenty of wear left in them.

CAPTAIN Just a moment. Do you mean to say the people of the neighborhood have seen my children wearing old curtains?

MARIA Oh, yes, they've become very popular. Everyone smiles at them.

CAPTAIN I don't wonder.

MARIA They say, "There go Captain von Trapp's children."

CAPTAIN My children have always been a credit to my name.

MARIA But, Captain, they weren't. They were just unhappy little marching machines.

CAPTAIN I don't care to hear from you about my children.

MARIA Well, you must hear from someone. You're not home long enough to know them.

CAPTAIN I said I don't want to hear—

MARIA I know you don't—but you've got to. Take Liesl— Liesl isn't a child any more. And if you keep treating her as one, Captain, you're going to have a mutiny on your hands. And Friedrich—Friedrich's afraid to be himself—he's shy—he's aloof, Friedrich needs you—he needs your confidence—

CAPTAIN Don't tell me about my son.

MARIA Brigitta could tell you about him. She could tell you a lot more if you got to know her, because she notices things. And she always tells the truth—especially when you don't want to hear it. Kurt—is sensitive—he's easily hurt—and you ignore him—you brush him aside the way you do all of them. (*The* CAPTAIN *starts to leave*) I haven't finished yet! Louisa—wants to have a good time. You've just got to let her have a good time. Marta—I don't know about yet —but someone has to find out about her. And little Gretl— just wants to be loved— Oh, please, Captain, love Gretl, love all of them. They need you.

CAPTAIN   Stop! Stop it! You will pack your things and return to the Abbey as soon as you can.

MARIA   I'm sorry. I shouldn't have said those things—not in the way I said them.

CAPTAIN   After you've gone there'll be—(*We hear the voices of the children singing offstage*) What's that?

CHILDREN (*Singing offstage*)
The hills are alive
With the sound of music,
With songs they have sung
For a thousand years.

MARIA   Singing.

CAPTAIN   Who's singing?

The hills fill my heart
With the sound of music—
My heart wants to sing
Every song it hears.

MARIA   Your children.

CAPTAIN   My children singing?

MARIA   I wanted them to sing for Frau Schraeder when they met her.

66

(ELSA *enters from the upper French windows, going to-ward the* CAPTAIN. *The children follow* ELSA *on, still singing,* FRIEDRICH *accompanying them on a guitar. They stand in a diagonal line in front of the French windows*)

ELSA Georg, you must hear—

CHILDREN (*Singing*)
   My heart wants to beat
   Like the wings
   Of the birds that rise
   From the lake to the trees,
   My heart wants to sigh
   Like a chime that flies
   From a church on a breeze.
      (*The* CAPTAIN *joins in the song*)

CAPTAIN *and* CHILDREN (*Singing*)
   I go to the hills
   When my heart is lonely,
   I know I will hear
   What I've heard before.
   My heart will be blessed
   With the sound of music
   And I'll sing once more.
      (*As the song finishes there is a moment of poignant silence.* GRETL, *who is carrying a white flower, looks to-ward* MARIA. MARIA *nods to her.* GRETL *goes to* ELSA, *curtsies, and hands her the flower*)

ELSA (*Touched*) Edelweiss! Georg, why haven't you told me how enchanting your children are?

67

(*The* CAPTAIN *goes to* GRETL *and puts his arm around her. He motions the other children to him. The younger ones surround him. He puts his other arm around* MARTA, *then reaches out and gently ruffles* KURT'S *hair. When he speaks it is not easy for him to control his voice*)

CAPTAIN Children, I'd like to have you show Frau Schraeder the gardens.

ELSA Yes, show me the gardens—(ELSA *and the children start off left, all talking simultaneously*) I want to see everything, and with you, too. I don't know any of your names yet, but it doesn't matter. I'm sure I won't get them straight for a long time.

LOUISA My name is Marta.

MARTA It is not. My name's Marta. She's Louisa.
(ELSA *and the children have disappeared*)

CAPTAIN (*Going to* MARIA) You were right. I don't know my own children.

MARIA They're waiting to know you. They want so much to. After I've gone . . .

CAPTAIN No. I want you to stay.

MARIA If I can be of any help.

CAPTAIN You have helped already. You have brought music back into my home. I had forgotten . . . (*Singing*)

68

To laugh like a brook
When it trips and falls
Over stones in its way—

BOTH

To sing through the night
Like a lark who is learning to pray—

I go to the hills
When my heart is lonely,
   (*He hands* MARIA LOUISA's *kerchief*)
I know I will hear
What I've heard before.
   (*The* CAPTAIN *takes the whistle from his pocket, shows it to* MARIA, *then throws it away*)
My heart will be blessed
With the sound of music—

CAPTAIN

And I'll sing once more.
   (*The* CAPTAIN *exits into the house.* MARIA *watches him go, smiles happily, then starts off, singing*)

MARIA

Doe—a deer, a female deer,
Ray—a drop of golden sun,
Me—a name I call myself,
Far—a long, long way to run—
   (ELSA *enters from the garden.* MARIA *sees her and stops singing*)

ELSA   I came back to congratulate you.

MARIA Thank you.

ELSA The Captain was really moved.

MARIA Yes, I think he was pleased. He's asked me to stay on
with the children.

ELSA Oh, you're staying on!

MARIA Until September.

ELSA September?

MARIA Then I go back to the Abbey.

ELSA The Abbey?

MARIA I'm going to be a nun.

ELSA Oh, how nice! (*She crosses to the table and sits*) When
you get back to the Abbey, think of us.

MARIA I'll pray for you.
(MARIA *exits to the garden.* ELSA *smiles to herself at the
expression of thoughtfulness, then her expression
changes as she realizes the prayers may be needed*)

Dim Out

Scene Ten

A hallway in the TRAPP *villa.*
GRETL *and* FRAU SCHMIDT *enter.* GRETL *bows to* FRAU SCHMIDT.

FRAU SCHMIDT No. (GRETL *curtsies*) That's right. You must do that to all the guests. (*Calling off*) Come along, children —the party's started.
    (MARTA *enters, going to* FRAU SCHMIDT)

MARTA Frau Schmidt, will you fix my bow? (FRAU SCHMIDT *reties* MARTA's *sash*) We never had a party in our house before.
    (BRIGITTA *enters, runs across the stage, and looks off.* LOUISA *enters.* LIESL *and* FRIEDRICH *enter.* LIESL *fixes* FRIEDRICH's *tie*)

FRAU SCHMIDT Oh, yes, there used to be lots of parties here.

LIESL Friedrich and I used to sneak out and watch them from the top of the stairs.

FRIEDRICH I remember the music.

FRAU SCHMIDT Once your father brought a Gypsy orchestra all the way from Budapest.

LIESL Yes, they wore red coats.

FRAU SCHMIDT Go ahead, children, and mind your manners. Come along.

(*She exits with* GRETL *and* MARTA)

FRIEDRICH I remember beautiful ladies and everybody laughing.

LOUISA (*Wistfully*) There was one lady—the most beautiful of all—I think she was here all the time.

LIESL (*Crossing to* LOUISA) Yes, Louisa.

BRIGITTA Can we dance while the guests are dancing?

LIESL Yes, of course. Remember what Fraulein Maria told us?

CHILDREN Yes.

(KURT *and* BRIGITTA *waltz together. So do* LOUISA *and* FRIEDRICH. LIESL *imagines a young man asking her to dance; she pretends surprise, then curtsies and extends her arms. Slowly she begins to waltz and is dancing gaily when the curtains part*)

Scene Eleven

The living room of the TRAPP *villa.*

The room is filled with waltzing couples, whom the children join briefly, before exiting. BARONESS ELBERFELD *is seated on the sofa, which has been pushed back. There are two men not dancing,* BARON ELBERFELD *and* HERR ZELLER. *They are obviously in a spirited argument. One couple stops dancing and goes to them as if to intervene. As the dance music ends we hear the angry voices of the two men.*

ZELLER You have German blood, haven't you?

ELBERFELD I am not a German. I'm an Austrian.

ZELLER There's going to be *Anschluss,* I warn you and everyone like you—and that goes for our—

FRAU ULLRICH Shhhh.

CAPTAIN (*Entering through the French windows and sensing a situation*) It's much more pleasant on the terrace. (*The guests, uneasy, start out to the terrace*) Elberfeld, it's very nice to have you and the Baroness here again.

BARONESS ELBERFELD Frau Schraeder's charming, Georg.

ELBERFELD I hope she isn't ill.
    (FRANZ *enters with a glass of brandy on a tray. He goes to the* CAPTAIN)

CAPTAIN Oh, no—just a headache. (*He takes the brandy from* FRANZ) I'm on my way up to get her. We'll find you on the terrace.

(*The* ELBERFELDS *exit. The* CAPTAIN *starts upstairs*)

BRIGITTA (*At foot of the steps*) Father, I don't think these people are having a very good time.

CAPTAIN I know, Brigitta, and it's your first party, too.

BRIGITTA Oh, I'm having a good time, even if they're not.

CAPTAIN Half the people I invited aren't speaking to the other half.

BRIGITTA Well, Father, maybe they're having a good time not speaking to each other.

(*The* CAPTAIN *smiles and continues up the stairs*)

FRAU SCHMIDT (*Entering on the balcony*) Oh, sir, Frau Schraeder asked me to let you know that she will join you in a few minutes.

CAPTAIN Thank you. You might see whether she would like this glass of brandy.

(FRAU SCHMIDT *exits.* KURT *and* MARIA *enter from the terrace, where we can see the guests dancing the Laendler, an Austrian folk dance*)

MARIA Kurt, I haven't danced the Laendler since I was a little girl.

74

KURT Oh, you remember it—show me—

MARIA No, I haven't danced since—
    (*The* CAPTAIN *has paused on the balcony and watches them*)

KURT Come, you said the left hand behind the back—

MARIA Yes, that's right. But first the boy and girl meet.

KURT Yes.
    (*He bows. She curtsies*)

MARIA Then they go for a little stroll.
    (*They join hands and cross the stage in a folk-dance step to the music coming from the terrace. When they reach the foot of the stairs they try to execute a movement which is a little awkward for* KURT)

CAPTAIN No, that's wrong, Kurt. Let me show you.
    (*He hurries down the stairs. He takes* MARIA's *hand and they continue the dance as* KURT *and* BRIGITTA *watch them. The dance reaches the point at which* MARIA *and the* CAPTAIN, *while holding hands, must execute a figure which calls for* MARIA *to turn under the* CAPTAIN's *arms and assume a position in which his arms are around her and his face close to hers. This physical embrace brings an awareness to both of them. When this same figure is repeated* MARIA *finds herself under the spell of an emotion that she has never experienced before and does not understand. In self-consciousness she*

75

breaks away. ELSA *has entered on the balcony and has taken in the situation*)

MARIA   I—I don't remember—any more.

CAPTAIN (*Also self-conscious*)   Well, Kurt—that's the way it's done.
(*The music comes to an end. The* CAPTAIN *exits to the terrace*)

BRIGITTA (*Crossing to* MARIA)   Your face is all red.

MARIA   I guess I'm not very used to dancing.

ELSA (*To* MARIA, *from the balcony*)   Well, hello there.

MARIA   Good evening, Frau Schraeder.
(*She exits.* ELSA *comes down the stairs*)

KURT   I hope you're feeling better, Frau Schraeder.

ELSA   Yes, thank you.
(KURT *exits.* MAX *and* FRANZ *enter through the front door.* MAX *is wearing a topcoat.* FRANZ *is carrying* MAX'S *bag.* MAX *puts his hands over* BRIGITTA'S *eyes*)

BRIGITTA   Hello, Uncle Max, we're having a party.
(FRANZ *exits upstairs with* MAX'S *bag*)

MAX   Good. Tell your father it's sure to be a success. I'm here.
(BRIGITTA *exits to the terrace*)

ELSA   Max!

76

MAX Elsa! Without a doubt you're the most beautiful corporation president in the entire world.
(*He kisses her hand*)

ELSA Thank you, Max.

CAPTAIN (*Entering from the terrace with* LIESL) Max—you're back! And as usual just in time for dinner.

MAX Georg, did you think you could give a gala without me?

CAPTAIN Oh, dear, now we have an odd man.

MAX A little odd, but charming.

CAPTAIN Liesl, run and ask Frau Schmidt to set two more places and tell Fraulein Maria I'd like to see her.
(LIESL *exits*)

ELSA Two places?

CAPTAIN We need another woman.

ELSA Who? Liesl?

CAPTAIN Oh, no—she's much too young. I'll ask Maria.

MAX You're not serious?

CAPTAIN But of course!

MAX She's a nursemaid!

CAPTAIN I don't think of her that way.

MAX I don't mind, but your friends—you can't ask them to dine with Maria.

CAPTAIN Why not?

MAX Elsa, tell him why not.

ELSA Max, you're talking like a royalist.

MAX That stops me. Being a royalist doesn't help you today.

ELSA Max, can you change in a hurry?

CAPTAIN Yes, Max, we can use you tonight.
     (MAX *hurries up the stairs*)

BRIGITTA (*Entering from the terrace*) Frau Schraeder, they're talking about you out there.

ELSA Come on, Georg, I've been dodging these people for an hour.
     (ELSA *and the* CAPTAIN *exit to the terrace*)

MARIA (*Entering onto the balcony as* MAX *reaches it*) Herr Detweiler, it's nice to see you again.

MAX Yes, you're going to.
     (*He exits.* MARIA *comes down the stairs*)

78

BRIGITTA I knew it all along. Frau Schraeder didn't have a headache. She just wanted to get out of the party. She was faking.

MARIA Brigitta, you shouldn't say things you don't know are true.

BRIGITTA But I do know. I heard her say to Father she'd been dodging these people.

MARIA That doesn't mean that she didn't have a headache. (*She speaks seriously*) It's very important that you children like Frau Schraeder.

BRIGITTA I like her all right. Why is it important?

MARIA Well—I think she's going to be your new mother.

BRIGITTA Oh, Fraulein, Father's never going to marry her! Why, he couldn't!

MARIA Why couldn't he?

BRIGITTA Because he's in love with you.

MARIA Now, Brigitta, that's just the kind of thing—
(*The full force of what* BRIGITTA *has said strikes* MARIA)

BRIGITTA You must know that.

MARIA (*In a whisper*) Brigitta—no!

79

BRIGITTA Remember the other night when we were all sitting on the floor singing the Edelweiss song he taught us? After we finished, you laughed at him for forgetting the words. He didn't forget the words. He just stopped singing to look at you. And when he speaks to you, the way his voice sounds—

(MARIA *can't accept an idea that conflicts with her commitment to the Church*)

MARIA No, Brigitta, no.

BRIGITTA And the way you looked at him just now when you were dancing. You're in love with him.

(MARIA *stands in stunned silence. The* CAPTAIN *enters from the terrace with* GRETL, LOUISA *and* KURT)

CAPTAIN One more dance, Gretl, and then to bed. (*He sees* MARIA *and goes to her*) Oh, Fraulein Maria, you're not going to have dinner with the children tonight. You're having dinner down here with us.

MARIA Oh, no! I can't.

CAPTAIN Oh, yes! It's all arranged. You'll have to hurry. You'll have to change. (*She starts up the stairs but stops as the* CAPTAIN *speaks*) Oh, and, Maria, wear the dress you wore the other night—when we were all singing. It was lovely—soft and white.

(MARIA *stares at him for a moment, then quickly exits upstairs.* FRANZ *enters from the dining room*)

FRANZ Shall I announce dinner, Captain?

ELSA (*Entering from the terrace, followed by the guests*) Oh, no, not yet. The children will want to say good night. Oh, Georg, I want the children to say good night the way they did last night.

CAPTAIN No, Elsa—not here—

ELSA Please, Georg, the way they did it for me—it was so sweet.

CAPTAIN No, no, not in front of strangers!

ELSA Please, Georg, for me.

MAX (*Entering onto the balcony, in evening clothes*) Presto chango!

ELSA Max, you're just in time. Children—now.
(MAX *comes down the steps and joins* ELSA *and the* CAPTAIN. *The children line up near the stairs. The guests assemble at the opposite side of the room. The children sing*)

CHILDREN (*Singing*)
There's a sad sort of clanging
From the clock in the hall
And the bells in the steeple, too,
And up in the nursery
An absurd little bird
Is popping out to say "coo-coo."
Regretfully they tell us
But firmly they compel us
To say "good-bye" to you . . .

So long, farewell,
Auf Wiedersehen, good night.

MARTA (*Steps forward*)
I hate to go and leave this pretty sight.
(MARTA *exits*)

CHILDREN
So long, farewell,
Auf Wiedersehen, adieu.

KURT (*Steps forward*)
Adieu, adieu,
To yieu, and yieu, and yieu.
(KURT *exits*)

CHILDREN
So long, farewell,
Au 'voir, auf Wiedersehen.

LIESL (*Steps forward*)
I'd like to stay and taste my first champagne.
(*To the* CAPTAIN, *speaking*)
No?

CAPTAIN (*Speaking*)   No!
(LIESL *exits*)

CHILDREN (*Singing*)
So long, farewell,
Auf Wiedersehen, good-bye.

FRIEDRICH (*Steps forward*)

I leave and heave a sigh and say good-bye,
Good-bye!

(FRIEDRICH *exits*)

BRIGITTA

I'm glad to go, I cannot tell a lie.

LOUISA

I flit, I float, I fleetly flee, I fly.

(BRIGITTA *and* LOUISA *exit together*)

GRETL (*Sitting on the bottom stair*)

The sun has gone to bed and so must I.

(*Still sitting she backs halfway up the steps one at a time*)

CHILDREN (*Having re-entered onto the balcony*)

So long, farewell, *auf Wiedersehen*, good-bye,
Good-bye . . . good-bye . . . good-bye.

(LIESL *goes down the steps to* GRETL, *takes* GRETL *in her arms and exits with the others*)

GUESTS (*Singing*)

Good-bye.

(FRANZ *announces dinner and the* CAPTAIN *and the guests drift off to the dining room.* MAX, *excited, goes to* ELSA)

MAX   Elsa, they're extraordinary!

ELSA   Fraulein Maria taught them to do it.

MAX I've been looking all over Austria for something like this for the Festival and I find it here.

ELSA Wait a minute, Max!

MAX A singing group of seven children in one family.

ELSA Max! Georg didn't even want them to sing in front of the guests tonight. I had to persuade him.

MAX Ah, then you have influence. You must talk to him.

ELSA Max!

MAX Elsa! This is important to Austria. And it wouldn't do me any harm.
> (*They exit into the dining room. The music segues into a slow, soft version of "The Lonely Goatherd." We see* MARIA *come down from the third floor onto the balcony. She is wearing the hat and dress she wore the day she first came to the villa and she is carrying her guitar case and bag. She makes sure the living room is empty. She comes slowly down the stairs. She looks unhappily toward the dining room, as though she wants to say good-bye to someone. She looks longingly upstairs, where the children have gone off. She takes a last farewell look around the room, then slowly and sadly exits to the outer corridor*)

Dim Out

Scene Twelve

A corridor in the Abbey.

SISTER SOPHIA *enters, accompanied by a young girl carrying a small traveling bag. She is distinctively and attractively dressed. They start down the corridor. From the opposite side six nuns enter in double file, chanting.*

NUNS

    Rex admirabilis,
    Et triumphator nobilis,
    Dulcedo ineffabilis,
    Totus desiderabilis,
    Totus desiderabilis.

      (SISTER SOPHIA *and the young girl watch the nuns as they go down the corridor and disappear. Then they exit*)

Dim Out

Scene Thirteen

The office of the MOTHER ABBESS.
The MOTHER ABBESS *is seated at her desk. The new* POSTU-
LANT *and* SISTER SOPHIA *stand facing her.*

MOTHER ABBESS Sister Sophia, take our new postulant to the
robing room. Bless you, my daughter. (*The* POSTULANT
kneels. The MOTHER ABBESS *blesses her. There is a knock on
the door*) Ave!
  (SISTER MARGARETTA *enters.* SISTER SOPHIA *and the new*
  POSTULANT *exit*)

MARGARETTA Maria has asked to see you. I know it has taken
her a long time.

MOTHER ABBESS I waited until she wanted to come to me.

MARGARETTA It's strange. She's happy to be here—but she's
unhappy too.

MOTHER ABBESS Why did they send her back—do you know?

MARGARETTA She doesn't speak. She hasn't spoken except in
prayer.

MOTHER ABBESS I shall see her.

MARGARETTA (*Crosses to the door*) Maria!
  (MARIA *enters, goes to the* MOTHER ABBESS, *and kneels*)

86

MOTHER ABBESS (*Blessing* MARIA) This must have been a trying experience for you.

MARIA (*Rising*) It was, Reverend Mother.

MOTHER ABBESS Has it taught you anything?

MARIA I've learned that I never want to leave these walls again.

MOTHER ABBESS Why did they send you back to us?

MARIA (*After a moment's hesitation*) They didn't send me back. I left. I left without telling them I was going, without saying good-bye.

MOTHER ABBESS Sit down, Maria.
    (MARIA *sits by the desk*)
Maria, what happened? Why did you do this?

MARIA I was frightened.

MOTHER ABBESS Frightened?

MARIA (*With difficulty*) I was confused. I felt—I never felt that way before. I couldn't stay—and I knew that here I would be away from it—that here I would be safe.

MOTHER ABBESS Maria, our Abbey is not to be used as an escape. What is it you can't face?

MARIA I can't face him again.

MOTHER ABBESS (*After a pause*) Thank you, Sister Margaretta. (SISTER MARGARETTA *exits. The* MOTHER ABBESS *stands behind* MARIA. *She puts her hands on* MARIA's *shoulders and speaks quietly*) Maria, are you in love with Captain von Trapp?

MARIA (*Torn*) I don't know. I don't know.

MOTHER ABBESS Tell me about it, my child.

MARIA (*With emotion*) Brigitta said that I was—and that her father was in love with me—and then there he was—and we were looking at each other—and I could hardly breathe. Then I knew I couldn't stay.
(*She rises*)

MOTHER ABBESS But you do like him, Maria?

MARIA I like the kindness in his eyes. I like the way he speaks —even when he's stern. I like the way he smiles at little Gretl.

MOTHER ABBESS Did you let him see how you felt?

MARIA (*Turning to her*) If I did I didn't know that I did. That's what's been torturing me. I was there on God's errand. To have asked for his love would have been wrong. I don't know, Mother. I do know this—(*She kneels before the* MOTHER ABBESS) I am ready at this very moment to take the vows of poverty, obedience and—chastity.

MOTHER ABBESS (*Helping* MARIA *to rise*) Maria, the love of a man and a woman is holy, too. The first time we talked

88

together—you told me that you remembered your father and mother before they died. Do you remember—were they happy?

MARIA Oh, yes, Mother, they were very happy.

MOTHER ABBESS Maria, you were born of their happiness, of their love. And, my child, you have a great capacity to love. What you must find out is—how does God want you to spend your love.
  (*The* MOTHER ABBESS *sits at her desk*)

MARIA I've pledged my life to God's service. I've pledged my life to God.

MOTHER ABBESS My daughter, if you love this man, it doesn't mean that you love God less. You must find out. You must go back.
  (MARIA *sinks at the* MOTHER ABBESS' *feet*)

MARIA Oh, no, Mother, please, don't ask me to do that. Please! Let me stay here.

MOTHER ABBESS These walls were not made to shut out problems. You have to face them. You have to find the life you were born to live.

MARIA How do I find it?

MOTHER ABBESS Look for it. (*She sings*)
    Climb every mountain,
    Search high and low,

Follow every byway,
Every path you know.

Climb every mountain,
Ford every stream,
Follow every rainbow
Till you find your dream.

A dream that will need all the love you can give
Every day of your life for as long as you live.

Climb every mountain,
Ford every stream,
Follow every rainbow
Till you find your dream.
  (*She lifts* MARIA *to her feet*)

A dream that will need all the love you can give
Every day of your life for as long as you live.

Climb every mountain,
Ford every stream,
Follow every rainbow
Till you find your dream.
  (*As the song swells to its finish* MARIA *removes the
  postulant's veil from her head and stands transfixed*)

Curtain

The VON TRAPPS at the Kaltzberg Festival Concert Hall

ACT TWO

Scene One

The terrace.
MAX, *blindfolded, and the children are playing blind-man's
bluff and singing.*

MAX (*Singing*)
   One little girl in a pale pink coat, heard

MARTA
   Layee odl, layee odl layee o

KURT
   She yodeled back to the lonely goatherd,

LOUISA
   Layee odl, layee odl o

ALL
   Soon her Mama with a gleaming gloat, heard

MAX
   Layee odl, layee odl layee o

GRETL
   What a duet for a girl and goatherd!
      (LIESL *pulls off* MAX's *blindfold*)

MAX
   Layee odl, layee odl o

ALL
  O ho, laydee odl lee o—
  (MAX *stops the singing*)

MAX Enough. Now sing seriously. Liesl, give us a key.
  (LIESL *picks up the guitar from the table and strikes a
  note*)

ALL (*Singing*)
  Do mi so do.

MAX That's nice—very nice—except it's no good. Imagine
that you're standing on the stage of a big concert hall.

LOUISA What concert hall, Uncle Max?

MAX Any concert hall—maybe Kaltzberg Concert Hall—but
a concert hall full of people. Now, once more.

ALL (*Singing*)
  Do mi so do.
  (MAX *stops them individually,* GRETL *last*)

MAX Gretl, why don't you sing loud?

GRETL I've got a sore finger.
  (*She holds up a bandaged finger*)

MAX (*Kissing her finger*) Now you can sing loud for Uncle
Max. The night of the party you sang so beautifully—with
such spirit. Well—let's try again. (*He gives them a down-
beat. They hit a chord. The* CAPTAIN *and* ELSA *enter from*

the garden. MAX *sees them and stops the singing*) They wanted to sing for me, the darlings, but they don't sing as well as they used to.

LOUISA We need Fraulein Maria.

CAPTAIN (*Taking the guitar from* LIESL) We do not need Fraulein Maria. You can sing just as well with me.

MAX But I've had experience with choirs, quartets, glee clubs—

CAPTAIN Max, please—(*To the children*) Now what would you like to sing? (*Singing*)
    Doe—a deer, a female deer—

KURT Fraulein Maria always started with—

CAPTAIN We are not to mention Fraulein Maria.

ELSA (*Sensing something*) Come on, Max, I feel like a brisk walk.

MAX That's just what I need—(*He follows her, turns*) Is anyone using the car?
    (MAX *and* ELSA *exit*)

CAPTAIN Now, what are you going to sing?
    (LIESL *starts and conducts the children*)

CHILDREN (*Singing*)
    The hills are alive
    With the sound of music,

95

(*The* CAPTAIN *joins the singing*)
With songs they have sung
For a thousand years.
(*The* CAPTAIN *stops*)

CAPTAIN No, not that—(*Leading* LOUISA *aside*) Louisa, did you play any of your tricks—any of your jokes—on Fraulein Maria?

LOUISA Only those she liked and laughed at.

CAPTAIN You didn't put toads in her bed?

LOUISA No, Father.

CAPTAIN Well, something must have happened—for her to leave us without even saying good-bye.

GRETL Isn't Fraulein Maria coming back?

CAPTAIN No, darling. I don't think so.

MARTA But she was the best governess we ever had.

CAPTAIN You're not going to have a governess any more.

LOUISA Oh, good!

KURT I'm not sure that's good.

CAPTAIN You're going to have a new mother.

96

LIESL A new mother?

FRIEDRICH Frau Schraeder?

CAPTAIN Yes. It was all settled last night. I'm very happy. Well
—it's time for your afternoon walk.
   (LIESL *kisses him. He hands her the guitar and exits
   into the house*)

LOUISA When Fraulein Maria wanted to feel better, she used
to sing that song—remember?

LIESL (*Putting the guitar on the table*) Yes.

BRIGITTA All right. Let's try it.

ALL (*Singing*)
   Raindrops on roses and whiskers on kittens,
   Bright copper kettles and warm woolen mittens.
   Brown paper packages tied up with strings—
   These are a few of my favorite things.
      (*They stop*)

GRETL Why don't I feel better?
   (*Offstage* MARIA *picks up the song*)

MARIA (*Singing offstage*)
   Girls in white dresses with blue satin sashes,
   Snowflakes that stay on my nose and eyelashes,
   Silver-white winters that melt into springs—
   These are a few of my favorite things.

CHILDREN Maria! Maria's back!
> (*They run to meet her as she enters. She is wearing the dress we saw the new* POSTULANT *wear.* FRIEDRICH *takes her suitcase and guitar and sets them above the stool*)

MARIA *and* CHILDREN (*Singing*)
> When the dog bites,
> When the bee stings,
> When I'm feeling sad,
> I simply remember my favorite things
> And then I don't feel so bad.

MARIA (*Hugging them*) Children, children, I'm so happy to see you. I must find your father right away.

MARTA I'll find him.
> (*She runs into the house*)

KURT I'll go with you.
> (*He follows* MARTA *into the house*)

MARIA (*To* GRETL) How's your sore finger?

GRETL You remembered!

MARIA Liesl—are you all right?

LIESL Yes, Fraulein, I'm all right.

MARIA Many telegrams lately?

LIESL No, Fraulein. Now I'll be glad to go to boarding school.

MARIA Liesl, you can't use boarding school to escape your problems. You have to face them. Oh, I have so much to talk to you about.

LOUISA We have some things to tell you, too.

MARIA You must have a great deal to tell me.

BRIGITTA I guess the most important thing is that Father's going to be married.

MARIA Married?

LOUISA To Frau Schraeder.

MARIA Are you sure?

BRIGITTA Oh, yes, he just told us—he told us himself.
    (KURT *and* MARTA *enter from the house*)

KURT We found him.
    (*The* CAPTAIN *enters from the house*)

CAPTAIN (*Significantly*) Liesl—

LIESL Louisa, Brigitta, boys! Maria, we'll be in the nursery.
    (*The children exit into house,* FRIEDRICH *taking* MARIA'S *bag*)

CAPTAIN You've come back?

MARIA Yes, Captain.

CAPTAIN You left us without any explanation whatsoever—without even saying good-bye.

MARIA It was very wrong of me. Forgive me.

CAPTAIN Why did you do this to us? Tell me.

MARIA Please don't ask me. Anyway, the reason no longer exists.
(*She picks up her guitar case*)

CAPTAIN Then you're back to stay?

MARIA Only until you can make arrangements for another governess.

CAPTAIN Oh, no! You've been missed by the children, I've missed—everybody missed you very much. Nothing was the same while you were away. Everything was wrong.

MARIA But I—

CAPTAIN We'll talk about it later. You go up to the children now.
(MARIA *starts toward the house*)

CAPTAIN Maria, a new dress?

MARIA We have a new postulant.
(*She exits into the house. The* CAPTAIN *sits at the table, picks up the guitar and strums it idly*)

ELSA (*Entering from the garden*) I know I'm right, Max. We'll find him and ask him.

MAX (*Following her on*) I'll take your word for it, Elsa.

ELSA Georg, settle this for Max and me, will you? How far down the mountain does your property go?

CAPTAIN (*Indicating*) Can you make out that stone wall? That's the property line.

ELSA (*To* MAX) You see.

MAX I didn't argue about it.

ELSA I know. That makes me furious. I don't like to win without a fight.
(FRANZ *enters from the house*)

FRANZ Herr Detweiler, while you were gone, you had a long-distance call from Berlin.

MAX (*Innocently*) Who could be calling me from Berlin?

FRANZ They said you'd know who it was.

MAX Oh, thank you, Franz. (FRANZ *exits into the house*. MAX *sits*) Georg, what were we just talking about?

CAPTAIN Max, this isn't the first call you've had from Berlin.

MAX Georg, you know I have no political convictions. Can I help it if other people have?

ELSA Let's not stir that up again. The Germans have promised not to invade Austria. Max knows that.

CAPTAIN Then why does he bother to answer those calls from Berlin?

MAX Because if they don't keep their promise, I want to have some friends among them.

ELSA Naturally.

CAPTAIN Oh, you agree, too?

MAX (*Rising*) Georg, this is the way I look at it. There was a man who was dying. They were giving him the last rites. They asked him, "Do you renounce the devil and all his works?" and he said, "At this moment, I prefer not to make any enemies."

ELSA Georg—if they—if they should invade us—would you defy them?

CAPTAIN . . . Yes.

MAX Do you realize what might happen to you? To your property?

ELSA To your children?

MAX To everyone close to you . . . to Elsa . . . to me!

CAPTAIN (*Rising*) Well, what will you do if they come?

102

MAX   What anyone with any sense would do—just sit tight and wait for it all to blow over.

CAPTAIN   And you think it will?

MAX   One thing is sure—nothing you can do will make any difference.

ELSA   Don't look so serious, darling. Take the world off your shoulders. Relax. (*The* CAPTAIN *sits and strums his guitar angrily.* ELSA *sings*)
You dear attractive dewy-eyed idealist,
Today you have to learn to be a realist.

MAX
You may be bent on doing deeds of derring-do
But up against a shark what can a herring do?

ELSA
Be wise, compromise!

CAPTAIN
Compromise, and be wise!

ELSA
Let them think you're on their side, be noncommittal.

CAPTAIN
I will not bow my head to the men I despise.

MAX
You won't have to bow your head, just stoop a little.
(*He stoops a little*)

THE SOUND OF MUSIC

ELSA

Why not learn to put your faith and your reliance
On an obvious and simple fact of science?

A crazy planet full of crazy people
Is somersaulting all around the sky,
And every time it turns another somersault,
Another day goes by!

And there's no way to stop it,
No there's no way to stop it,
No you can't stop it even if you try.
So I'm not going to worry,
No, I'm not going to worry,
Every time I see another day go by.

MAX

While somersaulting at a cockeyed angle,
We make a cockeyed circle round the sun.
And when we circle back to where we started from,
Another year has run.

MAX *and* **ELSA**

And there's no way to stop it,
No, there's no way to stop it
If the earth wants to roll around the sun!
You're a fool if you worry,
You're a fool if you worry
Over anything but little Number One!

CAPTAIN

That's you!

104

ELSA

That's I.

MAX

And I.

CAPTAIN

And me!
That all absorbing character!

ELSA

That fascinating creature!

MAX

That super-special feature—

ALL

Me!

CAPTAIN

So every star and every whirling planet,
And every constellation in the sky
Revolve around the center of the universe,
A lovely thing called I!

ALL

And there's no way to stop it,
No, there's no way to stop it,
And I know though I cannot tell you why.

CAPTAIN (*Speaking*) That's charming!

ALL (*Singing*)
>   That as long as I'm living,
>   Just as long as I'm living,
>   There'll be nothing else as wonderful as—

ELSA
>   I!

ALL
>   I—I—I
>   Nothing else as wonderful as I.

ELSA (*Speaking*) I . . . I . . . I . . .

CAPTAIN I! Me! On one thing alone we agree . . . each one is important to himself . . . but you can't save yourself by giving up, and you don't outwit a lion by putting your head—

FRANZ (*Entering from the house*) Your call from Berlin, sir.

CAPTAIN —in the lion's mouth.

MAX I'll call them back—

ELSA You might as well talk to them now, Max.

CAPTAIN Go, go.
>   (MAX *exits into the house followed by* FRANZ. ELSA *walks back and forth as she decides the situation must be faced*)

ELSA Georg—I feel I know what's going to happen here. Can't you see things my way?

CAPTAIN No—not if you're willing to see things their way. (ELSA *walks away. Her eyes go to the sunset on the mountains*)

ELSA There's one thing you do better here than we do in Vienna—your sunsets. I'm going to miss them.

MARIA (*Entering from the house*) Captain— Oh, I beg your pardon.

ELSA Maria! Georg, you didn't tell me Fraulein Maria was back. I'm delighted.

MARIA Thank you. Captain, the children would like to know whether they could take a holiday from their lessons tomorrow so that we can go on a picnic.

CAPTAIN Yes, I don't mind.

MARIA That will make them very happy. And may I be permitted to wish you happiness too, Frau Schraeder— Captain. The children have told me you're going to be married.

ELSA I'm afraid the children were wrong. (*She goes to the* CAPTAIN) Georg, I've got to finish my packing if I'm to get back to Vienna.

CAPTAIN If you feel you must. I'll tell Franz to have the car ready.

ELSA I can do that. *Auf Wiedersehen,* Georg. Good-bye, Maria.

> (*She exits into the house. The* CAPTAIN *turns and looks after her*)

MARIA I'm sorry if I said something I shouldn't have said.

CAPTAIN You did say the wrong thing—but you said it at the right time.

MARIA The children told me that you were going to marry Frau Schraeder.

CAPTAIN We found we just couldn't go the same way. That door is shut.

MARIA Sister Margaretta always says, "When God shuts a door—"

CAPTAIN I know—"He opens a window." Maria, why did you run away to the Abbey? . . . What made you come back?

MARIA The Mother Abbess—she said that you have to look for your life.

CAPTAIN Often when you find it, you don't recognize it.

MARIA No.

CAPTAIN Not at first. Then one day—one night—all of a sudden, it stands before you.

MARIA Yes.

CAPTAIN I look at you now, and I realize this is not something that has just happened. It's something I've known—deep inside me—for many weeks . . . You knew it, too! (*She nods*) What was it that told you?

MARIA Brigitta. She said—when we were dancing—that night—

CAPTAIN She was quite right. That was not just an ordinary dance, was it?

MARIA I hadn't danced since I was a very little girl. It's quite different after you're grown up, isn't it?

CAPTAIN When you were a very little girl, did a very little boy ever kiss you?

MARIA Uh-huh.

CAPTAIN That's quite different, too.

MARIA Is it? (*They kiss*) It *is* different.

CAPTAIN Your whole life will be different now, Maria. I'll take you anywhere you want to go—give you anything you wish.

MARIA But I don't want to go anywhere. All I could wish for is right here. (*She sings*)

An ordinary couple
Is all we'll ever be,
For all I want of living
Is to keep you close to me,
To laugh and weep together
While time goes on its flight,
To kiss you every morning
And to kiss you every night.
We'll meet our daily problems,
And rest when day is done,
Our arms around each other
In the fading sun.
An ordinary couple,
Across the years we'll ride,
Our arms around each other,
And our children by our side . . .
Our arms around each other.

CAPTAIN (*Speaking*) You know—those two ought to get together sometime.

MARIA Who?

CAPTAIN The Mother Abbess and Brigitta. (*He sings*)
An ordinary couple,
That's all we'll ever be,
For all I want of living
Is to keep you close to me,
To laugh and weep together
While time goes on its flight,
To kiss you every morning,
And to kiss you every night.

MARIA

> We'll meet our daily problems,
> And rest when day is done,
> Our arms around each other
> In the fading sun.

BOTH

> An ordinary couple,
> Across the years we'll ride,
> Our arms around each other,
> And our children by our side . . .
> Our arms around each other!

CAPTAIN (*Speaking*)   Maria, is there someone I should go to—
to ask permission to marry you?

MARIA   Why don't we ask the children?
> (*They exit into the house*)

Blackout

Scene Two

A corridor in the Abbey.

Three young postulants run on but stop short as they almost collide with four nuns who are crossing from the other direction. The postulants stand back with pretended meekness. Just before the nuns disappear two of them look back at the postulants with a quiet smile. The nuns exit. The postulants make sure they are gone, then run off in the opposite direction. Two other nuns enter carrying the MOTHER ABBESS' *ceremonial cape.* SISTER MARGARETTA *and* SISTER BERTHE *enter from the opposite side and accept the cape. The nuns exit. The* MOTHER ABBESS *enters.* SISTER MARGARETTA *and* SISTER BERTHE *solemnly put the cape on the* MOTHER ABBESS' *shoulders. The three raise their hands in silent prayer and then exit.*

Dim Out

The office of the MOTHER ABBESS.
*A small suitcase is open on a stool. As the lights come up
we see* MARIA, *center, being dressed for her wedding. Some of
the nuns are helping to put on and adjust the overskirt of her
wedding dress with its train. Two of the nuns put on her
veil. The* MOTHER ABBESS *enters, followed by* SISTER BERTHE *and*
SISTER MARGARETTA. *The* MOTHER ABBESS *goes to one side of*
MARIA, *the two sisters to the other side, and they stand admiring her.*

MARIA Reverend Mother, have I your permission to look at
myself? I brought a mirror. It's in my suitcase—

MOTHER ABBESS Sister Berthe!
(SISTER BERTHE *opens the suitcase and searches for the
mirror. She takes a sheer nightgown from the suitcase
and holds it up*)

SISTER BERTHE Sister Margaretta—isn't this a little—

SISTER MARGARETTA I don't think she's had time to put in the
linings.

MOTHER ABBESS Sister Berthe, the mirror.
(SISTER BERTHE *gives the mirror to* MARIA, *who looks at
herself*)

MARIA Why, Mother—I look—

MOTHER ABBESS Don't be vain, my daughter. Let me say it
for you. You are indeed beautiful, my dear.
>   (MARIA *returns the mirror to* SISTER BERTHE. SISTER SOPHIA
>   *hands a white prayer book to* MARIA. *A nun hands the*
>   MOTHER ABBESS *a wreath of myrtle.* MARIA *kneels as the*
>   MOTHER ABBESS *places this symbol of virginity on* MARIA'S
>   *head.* MARIA *moves forward to take her position for the
>   wedding march. The nuns break into a joyous chant*)

NUNS (*Singing*)
Gaudeamus omnes in Domino diem festum celebrantes.

Scene Four

A cloister overlooking the chapel.

The action continues uninterrupted from the preceding scene.

The metal grille is lowered between MARIA *and the nuns. Behind the nuns a drop is lowered suggesting the dome of a chapel.* MARIA *makes a gesture of farewell to the* MOTHER ABBESS. *The nuns line up behind the grille to watch the march to the altar and a ceremony of which they cannot be a part.*

The VON TRAPP *girls enter dressed for the wedding and take their places in front of* MARIA. LIESL *and* LOUISA *are in front, behind them are* BRIGITTA *and* MARTA, *then* GRETL *carrying a bouquet of roses. (The other girls carry small bouquets.)* KURT *enters, stands beside* MARIA, *and gives her his arm. From the other side* FRIEDRICH *enters, carrying a velvet pillow on which rests the* CAPTAIN'S *Navy hat. He is followed by* CAPTAIN VON TRAPP *in dress uniform, wearing his sword and decorations.*

The wedding march starts. The wedding procession moves to its solemn rhythm. Against the wedding march the nuns sing in counterpoint.

NUNS (*Singing*)
How do you solve a problem like Maria?
How do you catch a cloud and pin it down?
How do you find a word that means Maria?
A flibbertijibbet, a will-o'-the-wisp, a clown!
Many a thing you know you'd like to tell her,
Many a thing she ought to understand,

But how do you make her stay
And listen to all you say?
How do you keep a wave upon the sand?
How do you solve a problem like Maria?
How do you hold a moonbeam in your hand?

(*During the above chorus the girls and* MARIA *are crossing the stage. Just before they reach center, they stop.* GRETL *turns, curtsies to* MARIA, *and hands her the bouquet of roses.* KURT *leaves her side and stands with his back to the grille, where he is joined by* FRIEDRICH. *The procession starts again. The* CAPTAIN *takes his place beside* MARIA, *offering her his arm. The procession continues until it disappears offstage,* KURT *and* FRIEDRICH *falling into line behind the* CAPTAIN *and* MARIA. *The nuns come from either side of the grille, forming a line in front of it, the* MOTHER ABBESS *in the center. They sing joyfully*)

Confitemini Domino
Quoniam bonus, quoniam bonus,
Quoniam in saeculum misericordia ejus.

Alleluia

Gaudeamus omnes in Domino diem festum celebrantes.
(*The* MOTHER ABBESS *bows to the nuns and all exit*)

Dim Out

Scene Five

The living room.
As the curtains part, MAX *is on the balcony with some printed programs in his hand.*

MAX (*Coming down the steps*) Children, children! Liesl, Friedrich, Gretl, Kurt, Marta . . . See! Kaltzberg Festival, nineteen thirty-eight. (LIESL, BRIGITTA *and* GRETL *enter from the terrace.* MAX *holds up the programs*) Look here! The Trapp Family Singers! And here are all of your names . . . Liesl, Friedrich, Louisa, Kurt, Brigitta, Marta and Gretl.

GRETL Why am I always last?

LIESL Because you're the youngest.

MAX Liesl, I'm depending on you. Day after tomorrow you must all be ready at eleven o'clock in the morning. That's when—
  (FRAU SCHMIDT *enters from the terrace*)

FRAU SCHMIDT Herr Detweiler, can you help me, please? The Gauleiter is here. He wants to know why we aren't flying the new flag.
  (HERR ZELLER *enters from the terrace*)

ZELLER (*Saluting* MAX) Heil!

117

FRAU SCHMIDT I tried to explain—

ZELLER Keep quiet. (*To* MAX) When is Captain von Trapp returning?

MAX Who knows? When a man is on his honeymoon—

ZELLER These are not times for joking! It's been four days since the *Anschluss*. This is the only house in the province that is not flying the flag of the Third Reich.

BRIGITTA You mean the flag with the black spider on it?

MAX Brigitta!

ZELLER Do you permit such remarks in this house? Who are you?

MAX I am Maximilian Detweiler, First Secretary of the Ministry of Education and Culture.

ZELLER That was in the old regime.

MAX In the old regime I was Third Secretary. Now I'm First Secretary.

ZELLER Good! Then you will order them to fly the flag.

FRAU SCHMIDT Captain von Trapp wouldn't— I mean, I can take my orders only from Captain von Trapp.

ZELLER You will take your orders from us—and so will the Captain. (*To* MAX) Heil!

MAX (*Reluctantly*) Heil!
   (ZELLER *exits to the terrace*)

GRETL Why was he so cross?

FRAU SCHMIDT Everybody's cross these days.
   (*She exits*)

LIESL (*Going to* MAX) Is Father going to be in trouble?

MAX He doesn't have to be. The thing to do today is to get
along with everybody. Now, Liesl, be sure you get all the
children on the bus at eleven o'clock.

BRIGITTA Uncle Max, are you sure this is going to be all right
with Father?

MAX He'll be pleased and proud.

BRIGITTA Liesl, do you think so?

MAX Brigitta, don't you trust me?

BRIGITTA No.

MAX Well, anyway, the bus leaves at eleven o'clock.
   (FRANZ *enters from the front door, carrying two suit-
   cases*)

FRANZ Fraulein Liesl, see what I have here.

LIESL That's Father's luggage.

119

FRANZ   Yes, they're back.
(*He exits upstairs*)

MAX (*Nervously*)   Liesl, they'll have such a lot to tell us, let's not hurry about telling them anything.
(*The other children enter and they all run to the front door*)

CHILDREN   They're back, they're back!
(*The* CAPTAIN *and* MARIA *enter and are surrounded by the children*)

MARIA   Children! Max!

MAX   We didn't expect you back until next week.

CAPTAIN   Max, it's good you're here. There's much I want to know.

MARIA   Children, we missed you so very much.

GRETL   What did you miss most?

MARIA   We missed all that noise you make in the morning—

CAPTAIN   That noise you make telling each other to be quiet. We missed climbing upstairs to say good night to you.

MARIA   We missed hearing you sing.

BRIGITTA   You came back just in time to hear us sing. Look, Father, we're going to sing in the Kaltzberg Festival Friday night.
(*She shows him a program*)

THE SOUND OF MUSIC

CAPTAIN Let me see that. (*He looks at the program*) Max, are you responsible for this?

MAX I've just been waiting to talk to you about it, Georg.

CAPTAIN You can't talk your way out of this one.
 (FRANZ *and* FRAU SCHMIDT *enter from the front door with packages*)

FRIEDRICH Presents!

CHILDREN (*Taking the presents and running upstairs,* FRAU SCHMIDT *and* FRANZ *following them*)
 Give me mine.
 Where's mine?
 Let's open them in the nursery.
 Which one is mine?
  (*They exit, except for* LIESL, *who remains on the balcony*)

MAX Georg, I had to make a last minute decision—I was very fortunate to be able to enter them at all—they'll be the talk of the Festival—seven children in one family—

CAPTAIN Not my family!

MAX The committee heard them—they were enchanted.

MARIA Really, Max? What did they say?

MAX You never heard such praise.

MARIA Georg, did you hear—

CAPTAIN The Von Trapp family does not sing in public.

MARIA But if they make people happy—

MAX And for the Festival—people come from all over the world—

CAPTAIN It is out of the question!
    (*He starts for the stairs*)

MAX Georg, it's for Austria.

CAPTAIN There is no Austria!

MAX But the *Anschluss* happened peacefully. Let's at least be grateful for that.

CAPTAIN (*At the top of the stairs*) Grateful? To these swine?
    (*He exits.* LIESL *comes downstairs*)

MAX Maria, he must at least pretend to work with these people. I admire the way he feels—but you must convince him he has to compromise.

MARIA No, Max, no.

MAX Maria, you must.

MARIA Max, I can't ask Georg to be less than what he is.

122

MAX Then I'll talk to him. If these children don't sing in the Festival—well, it would be a reflection on Austria—and it wouldn't do me any good.
(*He exits*)

LIESL Maria, I've always known you loved us children. Now I know you love Father.

MARIA I do, Liesl. I love him very much.
(*The two sit on the sofa*)

LIESL How can you be sure?

MARIA Because I don't think first of myself any more. I think first of him. I know now how to spend my love. (*She sings*)
A bell is no bell till you ring it,
A song is no song till you sing it,
And love in your heart
    Wasn't put there to stay—
Love isn't love
    Till you give it away.

When you're sixteen, going on seventeen,
Waiting for life to start,
Somebody kind
Who touches your mind
Will suddenly touch your heart!

LIESL (*Singing*)
When that happens, after it happens,
Nothing is quite the same.
Somehow you know

You'll jump up and go
If ever he calls your name!

MARIA

Gone are your old ideas of life,
The old ideas grow dim—
Lo and behold! You're someone's wife
And you belong to him!
You may think this kind of adventure
Never may come to you . . .
Darling sixteen-going-on-seventeen,
Wait—a year—or two.

LIESL

I'll wait a year—

BOTH

or two!
(FRAU SCHMIDT *enters from the front door*)

FRAU SCHMIDT There's a telegram for the Captain.
(ROLF *has followed* FRAU SCHMIDT *on. She exits*)

LIESL Rolf! Rolf, I'd like you to meet my mother—my new
mother.

MARIA (*Rising and going to* ROLF) Rolf, I am glad to meet
you finally.

ROLF (*Coldly*) I have a telegram for Captain von Trapp.
(FRANZ *enters on the balcony and starts downstairs*)

MARIA *(To* ROLF) You stay here with Liesl. I'll take it to him.
   (She reaches for the telegram. He withholds it)

ROLF I'm under orders to make sure the Captain gets it.

MARIA I think you can trust me to give it to him.

ROLF I have my orders.

LIESL Silly, they're married.
   (ROLF *sees* FRANZ)

ROLF Oh, Franz! This telegram is to be delivered into the
   hands of Captain von Trapp.

FRANZ *(Saluting)* Heil!

ROLF Heil!
   (ROLF *returns the salute and gives* FRANZ *the telegram.*
   FRANZ *exits upstairs)*

LIESL *(Shocked)* Rolf!

MARIA Even Franz.

ROLF Yes, even Franz. Even me! Even everybody in Nonnberg except the great Captain von Trapp. If he knows what's
   good for him, he'll come over to the right side.

LIESL Rolf, don't talk like that.
   (FRANZ *re-enters onto the balcony and comes down the
   stairs)*

ROLF And if he doesn't, he'd better get out of the country—there are things that happen today to a man like that. He'd better get out quick. (LIESL *runs to* MARIA *and buries her head on* MARIA's *shoulder*) Cry all you want, but just remember what I said before it's too late. (*To* MARIA) And you remember too.
(*He exits, followed by* FRANZ)

MARIA Liesl—don't cry.

LIESL How could he turn on Father that way?

MARIA Liesl—maybe he wasn't threatening your father—maybe he was warning him.
(*The* CAPTAIN *enters onto the balcony, an open telegram in his hand*)

CAPTAIN Liesl—
(LIESL *runs out*)

MARIA What is it, Georg?

CAPTAIN (*Coming down the stairs*) I didn't think I would have to face a decision this soon. Berlin has offered me a commission in their Navy.

MARIA Well, Georg?

CAPTAIN I can't just brush this aside. I admit it would be exciting to have a ship under me again. And it would be a relief and a comfort to know that you and the children are safe. But—it also means— Please, Maria, help me!

MARIA Georg, whatever you decide, will be my decision.
(*They kiss*)

CAPTAIN Thank you. I know now I can't do it.

MARIA Of course not.

CAPTAIN We'll have to get out of Austria right away.

MARIA *You'll* have to leave tonight—now.

CAPTAIN Not without my family. And we can't just pick up
and leave. They'll be watching us. We'll have to plan—(*We
hear the doorbell*)—we'll have to have time.
(*Offstage we hear "Heil!" exchanged.* FRANZ *enters*)

FRANZ Sir—Admiral von Schreiber of the Navy of the Third
Reich is here to see you.

CAPTAIN Thank you, Franz. (FRANZ *exits*) They didn't give
us time.

MARIA Then we'll have to make time.

CAPTAIN I'll bring him in. We must be careful.
(*He exits.* MARIA *looks up in prayer. As she does so, she
notices the Festival program in her hand. It gives her
an idea. She starts upstairs*)

MAX (*Entering onto the balcony, followed by* LIESL) What's
happening? Storm troopers! That's what I was afraid of,
Maria.

127

MARIA (*On the balcony*) Max, stay with Georg. I need the children. Liesl, quickly, find the children. Quickly—
(MARIA *exits to the third floor.* MAX *hurries downstairs.* LIESL *exits from the balcony. The* CAPTAIN *enters with* AD- MIRAL VON SCHREIBER, *in naval uniform, and* ZELLER)

CAPTAIN This way, Admiral, we can talk in here. Admiral von Schreiber, may I present Herr Detweiler . . . Max, I think you know Herr Zeller. Would you gentlemen care to sit down?

ZELLER (*Coldly*) We are here on business.

VON SCHREIBER Captain von Trapp, a telegram was sent to you three days ago.

CAPTAIN I've just received it. I've been away. I've only been home half an hour.

MAX Captain von Trapp has just returned from his honey- moon, sir.

VON SCHREIBER Congratulations, Captain.

CAPTAIN Thank you, sir.

VON SCHREIBER Your record in the war is very well remem- bered by us, Captain.

CAPTAIN It's good to hear you say that, sir.

ZELLER Let's get to the point.

VON SCHREIBER (*To* ZELLER) If you don't mind. (*To the* CAP-TAIN) In our Navy we hold you in very high regard. That explains why I am here. Having had no answer to our telegram, the High Command has sent me in person.

CAPTAIN That's very flattering, Admiral. But I've had no time to consider—
  (MARIA *enters onto the balcony. She is carrying the Festival programs*)

VON SCHREIBER I am here to present you with your commission.

CAPTAIN I am deeply conscious of the honor, sir, but—

VON SCHREIBER And your orders to report immediately to the naval base at Bremerhaven—

MARIA (*Coming downstairs*) Immediately? Oh, I'm afraid that would be impossible for you, Georg.

CAPTAIN Admiral, may I present my wife, the Baroness von Trapp, Admiral von Schreiber.

VON SCHREIBER Madame!

MARIA (*To* VON SCHREIBER) What I meant sir, is that we are all singing in the Kaltzberg Festival Friday night. (*The children start entering onto the balcony*) You see—the Von Trapp Family Singers—here in the program. (*She hands programs to both* VON SCHREIBER *and* ZELLER)

129

MAX It's been arranged by the Ministry of Education and Culture.

VON SCHREIBER Friday night? This is Wednesday. That's only a matter of two days. It might be possible. You could report to Bremerhaven by Monday . . .

ZELLER Admiral!

VON SCHREIBER Is there a telephone I could use?

MAX (*Starting off*) This way, Admiral. If there is any question, perhaps adding the weight of my voice—
    (*They exit*)

ZELLER (*To the* CAPTAIN, *indicating the program*) It gives here only the names of the children.

CAPTAIN It says the Von Trapp Family Singers. I'm the head of the Von Trapp Family.

ZELLER It's hard to believe, Captain von Trapp—you singing in a concert.

CAPTAIN Herr Zeller, you may believe what you choose.

ZELLER It doesn't say here what you're going to sing. What are you going to sing, Captain?

CAPTAIN It's your privilege to come to the concert and hear us.

ZELLER I'd like to hear you sing now! Sing what you're going
to sing in the concert. Sing!

MARIA Do, re, mi, fa, so, la, ti— Liesl, will you give us a "do"?
(LIESL *blows a "do" on a pitch pipe*)

MARIA *and* CHILDREN (*Singing*)
  Doe—a deer, a female deer,
  Ray—a drop of golden sun,

MARIA
  Me—a name I call myself,

CAPTAIN
  Far—a long, long way to run . . .
  (*The music swells*)

Blackout

Scene Six

The stage of the Concert Hall, Kaltzberg.
As the lights come up and the music decreases in volume
we hear the voices of the VON TRAPP *family in a concert ar-*
rangement of "Do Re Mi." They are in concert position and
in Austrian folk costume. They are standing in front of the
velour curtain typical of a concert hall. There is a microphone,
left. The song ends. They accept the audience's applause. MAX
brings on the CAPTAIN'S *guitar.* MARIA *and the children sit on*
the floor. The CAPTAIN *sings.*

CAPTAIN
    Edelweiss, edelweiss,
    Ev'ry morning you greet me.
    Small and white, clean and bright,
    You look happy to meet me.
    Blossom of snow,
    May you bloom and grow,
    Bloom and grow forever—
    Edelweiss, edelweiss,
    Bless my homeland forever.

    Edelweiss, edelweiss,
    Every morning . . .
        (He is looking at MARIA *intently and stops singing)*

132

MARIA *and* CHILDREN (*Singing*)
Small and white, clean and bright—
(*The* CAPTAIN *picks up the song again*)

CAPTAIN
You look happy to meet me.
Blossom of snow,
May you bloom and grow,
Bloom and grow forever—
Edelweiss, edelweiss,
Bless my homeland forever.
(MAX *enters and addresses the applauding audience*)

MAX Thank you, ladies and gentlemen. Thank you. (*The
family starts off the stage.* MAX *stops them*) Just a moment.
I have an announcement that concerns you. (*Into the microphone*) Ladies and gentlemen, the Festival Concert has come
to its conclusion—except of course, we don't know what the
conclusion is going to be. The judges are putting their heads
together to arrive at their decision, and while we are waiting I think there should be an encore. It seems this may be
the last opportunity the Von Trapp family will have to sing
together for a long long time. (MARIA *and the* CAPTAIN *ex-
change a glance*) I have just been informed that Captain
von Trapp leaves immediately after the concert for his new
command in the naval forces of the Third Reich. A guard
of honor has arrived to escort him directly from this hall
to the naval base at Bremerhaven. (MAX *looks offstage, indicating the presence of the guard of honor*) And now,
ladies and gentlemen, the family Von Trapp again.

(*The* CAPTAIN *and* MARIA *confer briefly and hurriedly.
Then* MARIA *goes to the children and whispers some in-*

133

structions to them. They line up across the stage and
sing with a slight edge of apprehension)

MARIA

There's a sad sort of clanging
From the clock in the hall
And the bells in the steeple, too,
And up in the nursery
An absurd little bird
Is popping out to say "coo-coo."

CHILDREN

Coo-coo, coo-coo.

CAPTAIN

Regretfully they tell us
But firmly they compel us
To say "good-bye" to you.

ALL

So long, farewell, *auf Wiedersehen,* good night.

KURT *and* MARTA

We hate to go, and miss this pretty sight.
    (KURT *and* MARTA *exit, glancing back nervously*)

ALL

So long, farewell, *auf Wiedersehen, adieu.*

FRIEDRICH *and* LIESL

Adieu, adieu, to yieu and yieu and yieu.
    (FRIEDRICH *and* LIESL *exit*)

ALL

So long, farewell, *auf Wiedersehen,* good-bye.

LOUISA *and* BRIGITTA

We flit, we float, we fleetly flee, we fly.
(LOUISA *and* BRIGITTA *exit*)

ALL

So long, farewell, *auf Wiedersehen,* good-bye.

GRETL

The sun has gone to bed and so must I,
Good-bye!
(GRETL *exits*)

MARIA

Good-bye.

CAPTAIN

Good-bye.

BOTH

Good-bye.
(MARIA *takes the* CAPTAIN's *hand and they exit.* MAX
joins in the audience's applause and watches the VON
TRAPPS *off. Then he turns to see an envelope that is
being held out to him from offstage. He takes it and
goes to the microphone*)

MAX   Ladies and gentlemen, I have here the decisions of our
distinguished judges. We will start with the third award.

For this honor, the judges have named the trio of the *saengerbund* of Herwegen. (*The trio enters, bows, and exits*) The second award has been given to Fraulein Schweiger, the first soloist of the choir of St. Agathe's Church in Murbach. (FRAULEIN SCHWEIGER *enters, bows, and exits.* MAX *looks offstage, as if to reassure himself it is safe to proceed*) And the first prize—the highest musical honor in the Ostmark—goes to the family Von Trapp— (*The family* VON TRAPP *does not appear*) The family Von Trapp.
(*There is a commotion offstage*)

OFFSTAGE VOICES
Where are they—the Von Trapps?
They've gone!
Gone?
The Von Trapps!
Which way did they go?
Where are they?
Call the guard!
Hauptmann, take the first road! Ullrich, block the driveway!
Steinhardt, call district headquarters!
(*The commotion mounts*)

MAX (*To the orchestra*) Play something!
(*He exits hurriedly. The lights dim almost to blackness. Three men in SS uniforms run across the stage. Whistles and shouting voices are heard*)

Blackout

Scene Seven

The garden of Nonnberg Abbey.
The Abbey itself is on stage left, and there is a large single door opening from it into the garden. The rear wall of the garden has been hewn out of the mountain. It is low on stage left and rises sharply to a considerable height on stage right. At the rear of the rock wall of the garden a path starts about center stage and goes directly up the mountain. There is a wooden railing on the downstage side of the path.
At rise: The garden is in darkness. A few stars are seen in the black sky. What little moonlight there is discloses the shadows of the VON TRAPP *family huddled as if in hiding. They are wearing the native capes and hats. Their rucksacks are lying at their feet. The door from the Abbey opens stealthily and* SISTER MARGARETTA *slips through it, closing it behind her.*

MARGARETTA They've only five more rooms to search. It shouldn't be long now.

CAPTAIN How many of them are there?

MARGARETTA I counted only eight storm troopers and their officer.

MARIA Sister Margaretta, we didn't know we'd put the Abbey in this danger.

137

CAPTAIN It's outrageous. The church has always been sanctuary.

MARGARETTA Not with these people. This is the third time they've searched the Abbey.

VOICE (*Offstage*) Look there!
(*There is a frightened pause*)

MARGARETTA That's why we put you out here in the garden. They always search the inside—never the outside.

GRETL (*In full voice*) Isn't this God's house?

CAPTAIN Ssh! Yes, darling.

GRETL Then why did He let them in?

CAPTAIN Sh-h-h-h!

MARGARETTA (*To* GRETL) We must all be very very quiet. We'll let you know when they've gone.
(*She exits into the Abbey*)

MARTA After they've gone, can we go home?

CAPTAIN No, darling, we have a long drive ahead of us.
(LIESL *has drifted to the far side of the garden*)

MARIA Liesl, let's all stay close to each other.
(LIESL *starts back as the door opens suddenly.* ROLF *enters, dressed in SS uniform. He plays a flashlight across*)

138

the stage. The light first reveals MARIA. *The* CAPTAIN *starts toward* ROLF. ROLF *flashes the light on the* CAPTAIN'S *face, at the same time drawing his pistol. The* CAPTAIN *stops short*)

ROLF (*Calling over his shoulder*) Lieutenant! (*As* ROLF'S *head turns back his flashlight beams directly on the face of* LIESL. *There is a hushed moment as she looks pleadingly at* ROLF. *From a distance we hear the* LIEUTENANT'S *footsteps as he approaches. The sound draws nearer and nearer. Suddenly* ROLF *turns and calls through the door*) No one out here, sir!

LIEUTENANT'S VOICE (*Offstage*) All right! Come along!
(*The sound of the footsteps now indicates that the* LIEUTENANT *has turned and is walking away.* ROLF *takes one last look at* LIESL, *then exits, closing the door behind him.* LIESL *runs into her father's arms with a sob*)

CAPTAIN Sh-h-h! (*We hear the sound of an automobile starting. The family stands frozen. The sound fades into the distance*) Thank God!
(*The* MOTHER ABBESS *and* SISTER MARGARETTA *enter*)

MOTHER ABBESS They've gone!

CAPTAIN Reverend Mother, we're sorry we brought this on you.

MARIA Reverend Mother, we can never thank you.

CAPTAIN As soon as it's safe, we'll start. We hid our car deep in the woods.

MOTHER ABBESS The car will do you no good. They've left a guard on the road in front of the gate.

MARGARETTA I've been listening to the wireless. All the roads are blocked. The border's been closed.
  (*The* CAPTAIN *turns away and stands looking up at the mountains*)

CAPTAIN I've always thought of these mountains as my friends —standing there protecting us. Now they seem to have become my enemies.

MOTHER ABBESS Never your enemies. Haven't you read?—"I will lift up mine eyes unto the hills from whence cometh my help."

MARIA Georg, I know that mountain as well as I know this garden. And so do you. And once we're over that mountain, we're in Switzerland.

CAPTAIN But the children!

MARIA We can help them.

KURT Father, we can do it without help.

MOTHER ABBESS You'll have help. "For ye shall go out with joy, and be led forth with peace: the mountains and the hills shall break forth before you into singing . . ."
  (*The* MOTHER ABBESS *starts to sing*)
  Follow every rainbow
  Till you find your dream.

THE SOUND OF MUSIC

(The family, led by MARIA, *pick up their rucksacks, and put them on as they start out. The* CAPTAIN *picks up* GRETL. SISTER BERTHE *and* SISTER SOPHIA *enter and join the* MOTHER ABBESS *in singing)*

A dream that will need all the love you can give
Every day of your life for as long as you live.

(The other nuns come on and swell the volume of this chorus. We see MARIA, *followed by the children, start up the mountain path. At the rear is the* CAPTAIN, *with* GRETL *on his shoulders)*

Climb every mountain,
Ford every stream,
Follow every rainbow
Till you find your dream.

*(*MARIA *and the rest of the family are about to disappear along the path as*

The Curtain Falls